POTTED
HISTORY

POTTED HISTORY

How Houseplants Took Over Our Homes

CATHERINE HORWOOD

PIMPERNEL
PRESS LTD
www.pimpernelpress.com

Pimpernel Press Limited
www.pimpernelpress.com

Potted History
© Pimpernel Press Limited 2020
Text © Catherine Horwood 2007, 2020

First published in 2007 by Frances Lincoln Limited
This revised edition published in 2020 by Pimpernel
Press Limited

Design by Becky Clarke Design

A catalogue record for this book is available from the
British Library.

ISBN 978-1-910258-94-1
Ebook ISBN 978-1-910258-70-5

Typeset in Minion
Printed and bound in Great Britain
by Clays Ltd.

9 8 7 6 5 4 3 2 1

CONTENTS

7   Foreword

8   Introduction

12   Chapter 1 'A garden within doores'

20   Chapter 2 The arrival of 'exoticks'

28   Chapter 3 The chamber garden

38   Chapter 4 The fashion for forcing

48   Chapter 5 'Porcoipins for snowdrips'

58   Chapter 6 Town and villa

68   Chapter 7 'The largest hot-house in the world'

78   Chapter 8 *Flora domestica*

88   Chapter 9 *Rus in urbe*

100   Chapter 10 Gardens under glass

112   Chapter 11 Window gardens for the people

122   Chapter 12 Flower decorations

132   Chapter 13 'No home is complete without living plants'

142   Chapter 14 'Good for your health and good for your soul'

148   Conclusion

154   Plant lists

154   List 1: Plants introduced or discovered up to 1730

156   List 2: Plants introduced or discovered between 1730 and 1840

158   List 3: Plants introduced or discovered between 1840 and 1900

160   Endnotes

165   Bibliography

168   Index

176   Acknowledgements

IN MEMORY OF RICHARD GILBERT
(1924–2009)

FOREWORD TO REVISED EDITION

A surprising amount changed in the story of plants in the home since this book first appeared. In just twelve years, indoor plants have become status symbols with proud owners sharing pictures of their green treasures online almost as regularly as their cats, dogs and dinner plates.

What has caused this massive explosion in popularity? Three major factors are involved: improved propagation techniques leading to increased availability and lower prices, the changing lifestyles particularly of millennials, and the phenomenal growth of social media.

The new final chapter of the book looks at all these issues and draws some conclusions on what the future for houseplants might be.

Catherine Horwood

INTRODUCTION

At the start of the seventeenth century, Sir Hugh Platt, a successful horticultural author, published one of the first English books on gardening techniques. It was also the first to include a section on creating a 'garden within doores'.[1]

> I hold it for a most delicate and pleasing thing to have a faire gallery, great chamber or other lodging, that openeth fully upon the East or West sun, to be inwardly garnished with sweet hearbs and flowers, yea & fruit if it were possible.[2]

He recommended pots of carnations, rosemary, basil and sweet marjoram 'to stand loosely upon fair shelves'. Their heady scents were used to perfume the early modern home. Platt was not alone in getting pleasure from bringing plants indoors. In 1560, Levinus Lemnius, a visitor to Britain from Holland, had been forced to admit that 'altho we [the Dutch] do trimme up our parlours with greene boughs, freshe herbes or vine leaves, no nation does it more decently, more trimmely, nor more sightly than they doe in Englande.'[3]

The British love gardens and gardening so one might assume that we have always had a passion for houseplants. The truth is that our relationship with plants in the home has fluctuated, sometimes filling our rooms to bursting with greenery or scented plants, then banishing them on the grounds that they are unfashionable or too demanding.

Across the world, for thousands of years, plants have been brought into the home – for medicinal use, to cook with, for their scent, or just to admire. From the 3rd century BC, the Egyptians brought plants in clay vessels into inner courts for display. Fifteen hundred years before Christ, Egyptian Queen Hatsepshut grew Somalian frankincense trees in her temple. Terracotta plant pots have been found in the Minoan palace at Knossos on Crete. Roman villas were scented with the blossom of citrus trees.

Throughout medieval Europe cloisters housed tender herbs bred for both medicinal and culinary purposes. The first evidence of the English interest in half-hardy and tender plants is from 1338 when Edward III's Queen Philippa was sent plants of rosemary (*Rosmarinus officinalis*) from the Continent. In 1392 the Goodman of Paris (*Le Ménagier de Paris*) wrote that rosemary would not grow from seed in northern Europe but that there was an intriguing method for sending cuttings 'far away'.

> You must wrap the aforesaid branches in waxed cloth and sew them up and then smear the parcel outside with honey, and then powder with wheaten flower, and you may send them wheresover you will.[4]

But the history of plants in the English home is far more than just a list of plant introductions. It is interwoven with the stories of brave men who suffered months or years at sea and in unknown and often dangerous new territories to bring back new plant material for the ever more demanding collectors back home. It is the story of scientific curiosity, changing technologies and improved building techniques: how the layouts of houses altered and influenced which plants we could bring into our homes and how they could be displayed. Lighting and heating developments have been bad as well as good news for indoor plants: gas and coal fumes killed thousands of plants in the nineteenth century. Our late twentieth-century obsession with warmth through central heating has been just as damaging.

Just as fashions in garden design influenced which plants were found outside, so changing styles in interior design affected tastes in indoor planting. This was most obvious in grand homes where money was no object and fashions were followed more quickly. Under the Tudors, house designs changed from the dark, draughty baronial hall to a style more familiar to us now. This is when we find the first proof that plants were regularly brought into the home, and particularly the more modest home, which is how most of us live. Medieval coldness was gradually replaced by interior elegance. Later, Georgian minimalism gave way to Victorian clutter, only to be banished in turn by the early twentieth century's take on classicism. Post-Second World War tastes altered yet again as chain-store furnishing shops offered everyone the chance to buy Scandinavian-inspired designs. As a new century starts, television gardening and home make-over programmes compete to convince us that instant planting can transform our homes.

We are encouraged to think of the garden as another 'room', with doors opening out on to patios and terraces, conservatories attached to the house, and outdoor windowsills not quite part of the garden and yet best for growing plants that are hardy. For the most part, I have concentrated on the use of plants inside the house since plants in pots in the garden are another story. However, it is often impossible to disentangle the two across the centuries so where the stories cross over I have included them. For example, as domestic heating improved, plants that were originally thought suitable only for the hothouse moved to the conservatory, then into the main rooms of the house. Other plants once thought tender, such as the camellia, moved out into the garden.

So many plants for the home have arrived in Britain over the centuries, it would be impossible to tell the stories of all of them. Some – orchids and cacti for example – have thousands of varieties and need specialist care; vast books have been devoted to them.

This is not the story of flower arranging – that has also been told elsewhere – but again it is impossible to look at the history of plants in the home without considering the displays of flowers that often accompanied them. Cut flowers have always been brought into homes, since this is the simplest way of bringing a bit of the garden inside. But, just as potted plants require some skill to grow them successfully, so flower arranging also needs a different sort of artistic flair – sometimes highly stylized, sometimes just a question of popping a few flowers into a vase.

Today flowering plants are often treated in the same way as a bunch of flowers and thrown away when they have finished blooming. What a shame! Was it only the Victorians who had the time and enthusiasm to devote to conservatories full of potted plants? Most certainly not: over the centuries, the delight of having what seventeenth-century garden writer Sir Hugh Platt called 'a garden within doores' has captivated many. This is their story.

CHAPTER 1

'A GARDEN WITHIN DOORES'

In 1608 Sir Hugh Platt, flush with the success of his book for housewives, *Delights for Ladies to adorne their Persons, Tables, Closets, and distillatories with Beauties, banquets, perfumes and Waters*, a best-seller that ran for several editions, turned his hand to write about his great love, gardening. The result was *Floraes Paradise*, one the first gardening manuals and certainly the first to have a section on plants for inside the home.

Delights for Ladies had been packed with immensely practical advice on preserving food and distilling scented waters. Perhaps surprisingly for someone so interested in sweet smells, Platt, son of a wealthy brewer, had become an authority on soils and manures. Little is known about his own gardens in London's St Martin's Lane and on his estate near St Albans other than they were famous in their time. Platt was always keen to share his many ideas and inventions with a wider audience. Called 'the most ingenious husbandman of the age he lived in', in 1605 he was knighted by James I for his many mechanical inventions.

There was a good market for horticultural advice books. Platt's *Floraes Paradise* was reprinted forty-two years after his death, and retitled *The Garden of Eden*. Sir Hugh was full of opinions and advice for the budding indoor gardener.

> You must often set open your casements, especially in the day time, which would be also many in number; because flowers delight and prosper best in the open air.[1]

Where light was a problem, Sir Hugh recommended 'sweet Briers, Bays and Germander' as suitable for shady corners of a room. Come spring as the weather warmed up, empty fireplaces were to be filled with plants or flowers. Sir Hugh recommended that:

> In Sommer time, your chimney may be trimmed with a fine banke of moss, which may be wrought in workes beeing placed in earth, or with Orpin, or the white flower called *Everlasting*. And at either end, and in the middest, place one of your flower or Rosemarie

pottes, which you may once a week, or once every fortnight, expose now and then to the sun and rain, if they will not grow by watering them with rain water.[2]

Orpin (*Hylotelephium telephium*) was prized for its lasting qualities and so popular for indoor decoration. Ever the practical man, Sir Hugh suggested having removable sides and bottoms on wooden pots to allow for giving 'fresh earth when need is to the roots, and to remove the old and spent earth', and also to use a removable backing board so that 'the sun will reflect very strongly from them upon your flowers and herbs'. His most ingenious idea was a self-watering system for window boxes that used recycled rainwater and is surely worthy of any twenty-first century gardener's consideration.

From platforms of lead over your windows, rain may descend by small pipes, & so be conveyed to the roots of your herbs or flowers that grow in your windows. These pipes would have holes in the sides, for so much of as is within the earth, and also holes in the bottom, to let out the water where you please in great showers.[3]

Floraes Paradise contained plenty of suggestions for forcing plants to flower through the winter. This could be done in particular with roses and carnations, by placing them, explained Sir Hugh:

in a roome that may som way be kept warm, either with a dry fire, or with the steam of hot water conveyed by a pipe fastened to the cover of a pot, that is kept seething over some idle fire, now and then exposing them in a warme day, from 12 to two, in the sunne, or to the raine if it happen to rain, or if it raine not in convenient times, set your pots having holes in the bottom in pans of rainwater, and so moysten the roots.[4]

The popularity and timeliness of *Floraes Paradise* with its small section on 'a garden within doores' was to do with the fact that the layout of English living space had changed a great deal since medieval times. Within the early modern household, there was no concept of 'houseplants'. This did not mean that plants were not brought into the house. The apothecary had been using plants and flowers for medicinal potions and balms for centuries, cooks flavoured their dishes with a variety of herbs and housekeepers could not have been without plants to control pests that plagued every household. What was changing was the use of these plants in and around the home from the purely practical to the ornamental.

In 1560 Dutch traveller Levinus Lemnius wrote of his approval of the decoration of English homes:

> The neat cleanliness, the exquisite fineness, the pleasant and delightful furniture in every point for household, wonderfully rejoiced me; their chambers and parlours strawed with sweet herbs refreshed me; their nosegays finely intermingled with sundry sorts of fragrant flowers in their bedchambers and privy rooms with comfortable smell cheered me up and entirely delighted all my senses.[5]

The noble home no longer had the great hall where everyone from family and servants to guests had eaten. It had shrunk to become a still impressive entrance hall. The division between public and private family rooms had become clearer. Guests were entertained in reception or (with)drawing rooms which led off the hall. Families now ate in a room specifically set aside for dining while servants were banished for meals, retreating to the kitchen.

Fashions in house decoration had adapted to these changing layouts and uses. The ceilings and walls of grand houses were embellished with ornate plasterwork to make a show of wealth. Even a modest city merchant would aspire to have elaborate wood panelling in the main rooms of his house where his guests were received. Family plate was shown off on richly carved sideboards of English oak. William Harrison, in his description of England in 1577, noted that:

> In the houses of knights, gentlemen, merchantmen, and some other wealthy citizens, it is not [uncommon] to behold generally their great provision of tapestry, Turkey work, pewter, brass, fine linen, and thereto costly cupboards of plate ... now it is descended yet lower even unto the inferior artificers and many farmers, who ... have, for the most part, learned also to garnish their cupboards with plate, their joined beds with tapestry and silk hangings, and their tables with carpets and fine napery.[6]

Embroidered wall hangings were prized possessions. Fine carpets were more likely to be used to cover tables than to lie on stone or wooden floors. Heavy drapes cocooned four-poster beds. Curtains were still rare since windows were small and often shuttered to keep out the cold. Leaded panes of diamond-shaped glass let in little light through the hinged casement windows. Only the extremely grand could afford large windowpanes.

Away from the gaze of visiting guests, private family rooms were more simply furnished. Rooms were heated intermittently except for the kitchen, always the busiest space in the house. Few houses were connected to a water supply, so water had to be carried in from communal street pumps. In larger homes rainwater was collected for watering plants in the garden.

Garden styles also changed in the sixteenth century. After the breaking up of the monasteries, the enclosed style of the medieval period, the *hortus conclusus,* fell out of favour. It was replaced with a more outward-looking garden with lower walls and an intricate 'knot' pattern planting of box (*Buxus sempervirens*) and herbs. Even the humblest home had a utilitarian patch of ground for herbs, grown not just for cooking but also for a host of other uses such as medical treatments, insect repellents, household cleaners and, importantly, for strewing on floors.

One of the most commonly used herbs in the kitchen was common thyme (*Thymus vulgaris*), still widely used as a flavouring in cooking, unlike one of its many cousins, creeping thyme (*T. serpyllum*), which was thought to be unlucky to bring into the home. Another herb that had been found in England before the Norman Conquest, southernwood (*Artemisia abrotanum*), reputedly had aphrodisiac qualities if slipped underneath a pillow.

Rosemary (*Rosmarinus officinalis*), one of Platt's favourite plants for indoor cultivation, was also called 'guard-robe', with the recommendation that it be put into chests and presses among clothes to preserve them from moths and other vermin. Known also as 'dew of the sea', rosemary was much used during times of plague and was attached to walking sticks in pouches so that it was easy to sniff when passing through infected areas.

Sweet woodruff (*Galium odoratum*) was another herb used as an indoor insecticide under carpets and in linen cupboards. Also essential to any housewife's domestic armoury were the seeds of sweet cicely (*Myrrhis odorata*) crushed into furniture polish to give oak furniture an exotic fragrance of myrrh. But it was lavender (*Lavandula angustifolia*) that was the most widely used within the home and most widely grown in all the east coast counties, especially Norfolk where one of the last remaining lavender farms in England still flourishes.

Given the importance of plants such as these in any home for all their various uses, it is not surprising that herbs were grown in portable flowerpots as well as in formal outdoor gardens. In 1515 the gardener at Hampton Court spent 1*s.* 4*d.* on the transport of two lots of pots for herbs. Gervase Markham, writing in *The English Husbandman* in 1635, lists 'all sorts of Pot-hearbs'.[7] But since he talked of sowing herb seeds in the ground, here the meaning is herbs for the cooking pot. Herbs were also kept on kitchen windowsills to deter flies. While there is no evidence to support this, it is nice to think that, just as cooks today keep small pots of their favourite herbs such as mint, parsley and thyme on the kitchen windowsill especially during the winter months, keen early modern cooks also kept herbs in pots in or just outside the kitchen.

Most large households would have had a still-room for distilling cordial waters. This was also where herbs and flower stems were hung up to dry. Every housewife had her favourite recipes for distilling plant leaves and petals for medicinal purposes and scented waters – and, for extra inspiration, possibly a copy of Platt's *Delights for Ladies*. The still-room of Grace, Lady Mildmay (*c.*1552–1620) contained thirty-one bottles of oils and cordials. One of her recipes for a balm needed 159 different seeds, spices, roots and gums.

By the seventeenth century, many of the plants used in the home had been in Britain for at least 400 years. The rose has a long history across Europe. Wild roses, or briars, were native to England well before the better-known and more heavily scented roses such as *Rosa gallica* (now *R. gallica* var. *officinalis*) and the delicious *R. damascena* used to make attar (or oil) of roses. Ten thousand pounds of petals are needed to make half a kilogram of rose oil but only a tiny amount of the oil created delicious scented waters.

Given the basic sanitary arrangements endured by all, it is not surprising that royalty were the first to be supplied with scented flowers and plants. The royal gardeners' responsibility went much further than just tending the outdoor formal gardens of the palaces. John Lovell, who gardened for Henry VIII at Richmond, was expected to supply the king's table not only with fruit, nuts and scented water or distillations, but also with flowers. Professional distillers such as the Kraunckwells were paid £40 in one year to supply Elizabeth I with scented water. In addition, they received £25 for making herb bowers.

But a love of flowers was not restricted to royalty. In towns and cities, 'the pleasure garden', or outdoor flower garden, was often linked to the house by a terrace. Just as now, the suburban garden was seen as an extension of living space. Homeowners were encouraged to 'let open their Casements into a most delicate Garden and Orchard, whereby they may not only see that, wherein they are so much delighted, but also to give fresh, sweet, and pleasant air to their Galleries and Chambers'.[8]

'Fresh, sweet, and pleasant air' was important in the Elizabethan home. This was, after all, still a time when tussie-mussies (scented posies) and pomanders were needed as much within one's own household as on the streets to combat noxious smells. *Lavandula angustifolia*, English lavender or Lavender spike, was an essential ingredient of 'sweet bags'. These contained 'pot pourri', from the French term for rotten stew, used to protect clothes from insects. They were also hung from furniture to scent living rooms. In early modern Europe, perfuming clothes, especially linen, was seen as more important than washing the body. Lavender represented not just sweet smells but cleanliness as well, as the Latin root of its name – *lavare*, to wash – hints at. A recipe from *A Book of Fruits and Flowers* in 1653 had the added bonus of producing scented water:

> Take Damask Rose leaves, Bay leaves, Lavender tops, sweet Marjoram tops, Ireos powder, Damask powder, and a little Musk first dissolved in sweet water, put the Rose leaves and herbs into a Basin, and sprinkle a quarter of a pint of Rose water among them, and stirring them all together, cover the Basin close with a dish, and let them stand so covered, all night, in the morning Distil them, so shall you have at once an excellent sweet water, and a very fine sweet Cake to lay among your finest linen.[9]

Oranges were commonly used as the basis for cloved pomanders, the fruit spiked with cloves, rolled in orris root (*Iris florentina*) and dried. Cardinal Wolsey carried another variation on his journey to Parliament each day: 'a very fair orange, whereof the meat or substance within was taken out, and filled up again with the part of a sponge, wherein was vinegar, and other confections against the pestilent air; the which he most commonly smelt unto, passing among the press, or else when he was pestered with many suitors'. [10]

With scent so important in the home, it is not surprising that rare sightings of plants in paintings of early modern interior scenes often turn out to be that most deliciously perfumed plant, the carnation. With its stems covered in open flowers and expectant buds, it was brought inside for the delight of its delicate beauty and heady scent. There is a story that the seeds for both the wild carnation (*Dianthus caryophyllus*) and the sweet-smelling wallflower (*Erysimum cheiri*) were brought over from Caen in France lodged in the stones used to build the castles of William the Conqueror. By Shakespeare's time, the 'gillyflower' and its cousin, the common pink (*Dianthus plumarius*), were thought of as 'native' English plants.

Because of the need for sweet-smelling plants for inside the home, gardeners of grand houses were expected to be able not only to 'tread out knots in the quarters of Arms and fine devises' but also 'to set and sow in them sweet smelling flowers and strewing herbs'.[11]

Similar words were written by Thomas Tusser (c.1524–1580), a failed Elizabethan farmer but successful poet from Rivenhall in Essex. His book, *Five Hundred Points of Good Husbandry*, written in verse, ran to eighteen editions between 1557 and 1599, and is claimed to have been the most widely read book of poetry of the time. In it, Tusser emphasized that it was the wife's duty to supply flowers for the house:

In March, May and April from morning to night
In sowing and setting good housewives delight
To have in a garden or other like plot,
To trim up their house and to furnish their pot.[12]

In the long run, Tusser's verses gave Shakespeare nothing to worry about. In addition to ideas for 'trimming up their houses' and 'furnishing their pot', Tusser listed twenty-one 'strewing herbs of all sorts' which included basil, camomile, cowslips, sweet fennel, germander, hyssop, lavender, cotton lavender, marjoram, pennyroyal, various roses, sage, tansy, violets and winter savoury.

He also listed forty 'herbs, branches, and flowers for windows'. In addition to bulbs such as 'Flower de Luce' (*Iris*), 'Daffadondillies' (*Narcissus*) and 'Lillium Convallium' (*Convallaria majalis*), he included hardy garden flowers such as 'Columbines' (*Aquilegia vulgaris*), 'Holyoaks' (hollyhocks), 'Paggles' (*Primula veris*) together with shrubbier plants such as 'Bays' (*Laurus nobilis*), 'Lavender of all sorts' and rosemary. Three sorts of gillyflower were recommended for scent: queen's (*Hesperis matronalis*), stock (*Matthiola incana*) and wallflower (*Erysimum cheiri*).

We cannot know for certain whether these plants were being suggested for growing inside or outside the windows. If they were for indoors, they may have been cut into a bunch for displaying in vases on windowsills. Window boxes were available lined and sealed with pitch to make them watertight, and Elizabeth I was regularly supplied with plants, as opposed to flowers, for her windows. It was Sir Hugh Platt again who first mentions window boxes in 1594 in *The Jewell House of Art and Nature*. The writings of Platt and Tusser confirm is that in spite of a few new 'exotick' introductions, only 'native' or hardy garden plants were on show inside or outside the windows of British homes.

CHAPTER 2

THE ARRIVAL OF 'EXOTICKS'

Tender or 'exotick' plants that had to be overwintered indoors were status symbols for the rich and famous in the early modern period. The term 'exotick' was first recorded in 1597 in Gerard's *Herball*. John Gerard (1545–1612) was an early plant enthusiast best known for this *Herball*, a collection of 1,800 woodcuts describing plants already grown in Britain. Gerard delighted in the 'strange herbs, plants and annual fruits [that] are daily brought unto us from the Indies, Americas, Taprobane [Ceylon], Canary Isles, and all parts of the world'.[1]

While the plants grown by Gerard in his London garden in Holborn included many tender species such as abutilon, hibiscus and oleander, he did not tell us if he ever brought them into the house for shelter or decoration. Sir John Verney, however, makes this quite clear when instructing his gardener to plant his 'new tuberose roots into handsome Potts'. Sir John wanted not only to enjoy the perfume of this plant but also show off his tuberose (*Polianthes tuberosa*) so that 'when they are blowne [blooming] I may have 'em within doores'.[2]

Verney's tuberose was just one of many new exciting arrivals in the seventeenth century, having been brought from South America in 1629. World exploration was opening up new continents. Plant discoveries were arriving from continental Europe and the New World, brought home by sea captains and adventurers. Of the several thousands of varieties of plants introduced to Britain, many were tender plants thought not able to survive the temperate climate of England.

Plant collectors such as the John Tradescants, father and son, began changing the look of British gardens with their introductions, especially from newly acquired overseas possessions on the east coast of America. The Tradescants are the best known of the early plant collectors, a fame due in part to the ubiquity of one of John Tradescant the Elder's early discoveries from the newly opened-up continent of America, named after him by Linnaeus, *Tradescantia virginiana*. In the words of John Parkinson, his friend and neighbour in Lambeth and himself an esteemed gardener, Tradescant was a 'worthy, curious and diligent searcher and preserver of all natures rarities and varieties'.[3]

John Tradescant [the Elder] (d. 1638) travelled extensively across continental Europe and Russia in addition to his visits to America, from where he brought back varieties of lupin, phlox and centaurea, now all much loved English garden plants. According to Parkinson, Tradescant discovered many exotics including the wild pomegranate, which 'was never seene in England, before John Tradescante . . . brought from parts beyond the Seas, and planted it in his Lords [Edward, Baron Wotton] Garden at Canterbury'.[4]

Tradescant, then gardener to the Cecil fmaily at Hatfield House, also travelled to Paris on a plant-buying expedition, obtaining oleander, myrtle, fig, pomegranate and one-year-old orange trees in pots, which had cost him 10s. each, expensive considering he had had to pay only 2s. for a pear tree. Tradescant was willing to pay high prices for orange trees in pots since they were still one of the most sought-after plants of the period. His son, John the Younger (d. 1662), followed his father as a botanical explorer, particularly in the New World. Samuel Hartlib wrote in 1650 that he 'daily raises new and curious things'.[5]

Citrus fruit trees were among the most popular of the tender plants, but almost exclusively among the wealthy classes. A collection of them enabled courtiers to curry favour with their king or queen by presenting them with exotic fruits such as oranges. There is a delightful suggestion, probably apocryphal, that Sir Walter Raleigh introduced the orange to England by bringing back pips on one of his many journeys. Like many long-distance travellers, Sir Walter Raleigh returned with presents for his family. It is well known that he brought back the tomato and more dubiously tobacco. Less well known is that he gave his uncle-in-law, Sir Francis Carew, a seemingly small gift of orange pips in the late sixteenth century after a long voyage to the New World. A thoughtful man, Sir Walter knew that Sir Francis was a passionate gardener and desperate to try and grow the latest botanical finds from distant countries in his Surrey home at Beddington.

Oranges had been seen in England as early as the thirteenth century when some had been sent from Spain as a present from Edward I to his wife Eleanor of Castile. According to the queen's 'Wardrobe Book', kept in the Tower of London, she had been presented with a basket of Seville figs, a bale of dates, 230 pomegranates, fifteen citrons and seven oranges shipped from her native country to Portsmouth.

Although a poem celebrating a pageant dedicated to the arrival of Henry VI in London in 1431 speaks of orange and lemon trees laden with fruit, there is no record of anyone attempting to grow orange trees in England until the sixteenth century. Yet while wars hampered the delivery of these exotic fruits from countries such as Portugal, seafaring adventurers were in a prime position to bring back seeds of new plants. By the 1590s, in the grandest of houses such as those belonging to the Cecil and the Carew families, citrus trees were not just grown for their fruit but also regularly brought into the home for their deliciously sweet scent.

Sir Francis Carew's interest in plants was not unusual. It was seen to be part of a gentleman's education and duty to be involved in following botanical developments. This natural curiosity was the forerunner to the scientific discoveries of the seventeenth century. It encouraged rivalry between landowners who vied with each other over horticultural trophies.

William Cecil, later Lord Burghley, was a political grandee who also took a keen interest in his garden. In 1562 Burghley wrote to Sir Thomas Windebank, who was in Paris keeping an eye on Cecil's elder son, Thomas, after he heard that Francis Carew 'meaneth to send home certen orege pomegranat lymon and myrt trees'. Burghley could not resist at least matching Carew's order and gave Windebank a shopping list of horticultural desires.

I have alredy an orrege tree, and if ye price be not much, I pray you procure for me a lymon, a pomegranat, and a myrt tree, and help that they may be sent home to London with Mr Caroo's trees, and before hand send me in wryting a perfect declaration how they ought to be used kept and ordered.[6]

Such one-upmanship did not come cheap. A speedy reply from Sir Thomas confirmed his purchase of 'a lymmon tree and 2 myrte trees in 2 pottes, which cost me bothe a crowne, and the lymmon tree 15 crowns, wherein Sir, if I have bestowed more than perhaps you will at the first like, yet it is the best chepe that we colde get it'.[7] We do not know what Burghley thought of Windebank's purchases but as with any keen gardener anxious to get the latest fancy, price is rarely an issue.

Growing orange trees (rather than just eating the imported fruit) in England in the seventeenth century was still a rich man's sport. As garden writer John Rea noted in 1665, 'although the [orange] tree be rare and strange to many, the fruit is common and well known to all.'[8]

Less illustrious households may not have had the wherewithal to afford expensive citrus plants but this did not stop lesser families from having plants scattered throughout the home. In 1677, the agrarian writer John Worlidge (or Woolridge) claimed that 'scarce an Ingenious Citizen that by his confinement to a Shop, being denied the privilege of having a real Garden, but hath his boxes, pots or other receptacles for Flowers, Plants, etc'.[9]

While the fashion for flower-strewn floors had faded as more sophisticated floor coverings such as rugs from Asia and Northern Africa became available, scent was still needed and much prized in the home. Wallflowers were recommended by the herbalist and plant collector John Parkinson (1567–1650) to 'deck up houses'.[10] There was still a great belief in the medicinal powers of scented herbs. Diary entries by John Milton's daughter Deborah recall the family's hurried departure from London during the plague of 1665. 'The whole house smells of aromatick Herbs, we have burnt soe many of late for fumigation,' she wrote anxiously.[11]

The passion for plants was not restricted to growing them. Representations of flowers abounded, however limited the space. Worlidge described the flower-strewn paintings and embroideries that brought the garden inside all year round:

> In imitation of it, what curious Representations of Banquets of Fruits, Flower pots, Gardens and such like are painted to the life to please the Eyes and satisfy the fancy of such that either cannot obtain the Felicity of enjoying them in reality, or to supply the defect that winter annually brings.[12]

Although we know that living plants were taken into the home, it is still surprisingly hard to find paintings of interiors with clearly visible plants from this period. There is no shortage of paintings of ebullient flower displays such as those by Jan Breughel the Elder (1568–1625). These are extremely accurate depictions of the flowers grown at the time of the painting, though not necessarily all from the same season. But to find plants rather than cut flowers one sometimes has to look in unexpected places.

The Somerset House Conference (National Portrait Gallery, London) is best known as a depiction of the eleven men brought together to draw up the peace treaty between England and Spain in 1604, but it has a fascination for plant historians as well. Art historians may debate the identity of the artist or artists and marvel at the quality of the Anatolian table carpet in the two known extant versions, but for anyone on the trail of the history of plants indoors, it is the rambling shrub that can be seen behind the English delegation that is the most intriguing aspect of this painting. We cannot see clearly what species the shrub is or what it is grown in, but it is most definitely growing inside the room in front of the paned glass windows and provides a screen of greenery behind the English negotiating team.

Could it have its roots outside and have been trained in through an opening? This was a practice suggested by Sir Hugh Platt: 'You may also plant vines without the walls, which being let in at quarrels . . . may run about the sides of your windowes, all over the seeling of your roomes.'[13] This is unlikely, however, since although one window is open, it can be seen clearly that the shrub is not growing through it. Also the group is high up in the building, judging from the rooftops and chimneys that can be seen through the window.

Where did people go to buy plants for their homes? The first reference to a 'nurseryman' in the commercial sense does not appear until 1670, although the term 'nursery' referring to a place to grow young plants goes back to the middle of the sixteenth century. In London, the burgeoning trade in seeds and plants prompted nurserymen to band together in 1605, and form the Gardeners' Company which was given a Royal Charter two years later. By 1616, a second charter brought in seven-year apprenticeships, thus regulating who could and could not sell seeds and plants.

Plant prices varied enormously just as they still do. Seed of Canterbury bells (*Campanula medium*) could be bought for 9*d.* per ounce, narcissus bulbs cost 4*s.* for 100 mixed but 16*s.* 8*d.* for the best varieties. As always, tender citrus trees were the most expensive at £1 10*s.* to £3 each, which put them out of the reach of most at a time when a live-in gardener's wage was around 10*s.* a month. Few nurserymen specialized and certainly none in plants for the home.

In the first decade of the seventeenth century, there was a well-established garden just west of the City of London in Long Acre, which belonged to John Parkinson. Parkinson was apothecary to James I and was later appointed *Botanicum Regius Primarius* by Charles I. Although a pious man, he clearly thought he had a sense of humour since the title of his first book, *Paradisi in sole paradisus terrestris* (1629), translates as a pun on his name, 'Park-in-sun's earthly paradise'.

We do not know how big Parkinson's garden in Long Acre was but, judging from the large number of plants he grew, it was at least an acre in size. In particular, he grew many exotics especially from the Mediterranean countries. New finds were beginning to arrive in much larger numbers than in previous centuries. In 1607–8, Parkinson received over 200 different plants from an expedition to Spain and Portugal, only a quarter of which he listed in his catalogue. Some he found tender such as *Hibiscus syriacus*. He found it 'would not be suffered to be uncovered in the Winter time, or yet abroad in the Garden, but kept in a large pot or tube in the house or in a warme cellar, if you would have them thrive'.[14] Parkinson also grew *Bassia scoparia* f. *tricholphylla* (summer cypress), which, he noted, came from Italy where it was planted 'not only in their Gardens, but likewise in pots to furnish their Windowes'. In England it was mainly grown in pots 'to be placed in halls, chimnies, courtyards and the like'.[15]

The first simple purpose-built frost-free orangeries were built to over-winter delicate and highly prized citrus plants. While Francis Carew perfected the art of growing orange trees outside by using protective boxes around them in the winter months, the most popular way to grow them was in pots, enabling them to be brought indoors and given winter protection. At Burghley, where Cecil would have received his prize trees from Paris, a long room with windows all down one side is still known as the 'Orange Court' because of its long association with overwintering the precious trees.

Parkinson was well aware of the problems of growing tender plants without an indoor building or room to protect them during the winter months, as this excerpt from *Paradisi* shows:

> I bring to your consideration the Orenge alone without mentioning the Citron or Lemmon trees, in regard of the experience we have seen made of them in divers places. For the Orange tree hath abided with some extraordinary looking [after it] and tending of it, when as neither of the other would by any means be preserved any long time . . . Some keepe in great square boxes and lift them to and fro by iron hooks in the sides . . . to place them in an house or close gallery in for the winter time . . . but no tent or meane provision will preserve them.[16]

John Evelyn (1620–1706), diarist and passionate horticulturalist, counselled care in his *Kalendarium Hortense: or, The Gard'ners Almanac* in 1664, to 'retire your choicest greens and rarest plants (being dry) as Oranges, Lemons, . . . into your Conservatory' by the end of September.[17] Evelyn later paid the penalty of 'frost and rigorous weather' during the severe winter weather of 1684 'where [he] found many Greenes and rare plants utterly destroyed: The Orangs & Myrtils very sick'.[18]

'Greens' was the term used until the twentieth century to describe what we now call 'evergreens': that is, plants that do not lose their leaves in winter. Many of these were thought to be tender and need extra protection and may have been kept inside for most of the year. Worlidge mentions that 'greens' were available 'from the great Conserver of these Rarities, Mr George Ricketts of Hoxton'.[19] This term is also the origin of the word 'greenhouse' as somewhere sheltered to store tender plants. Evelyn is credited in the *Oxford English Dictionary* with first using the words 'greenhouse' and 'conservatory'. From mentions in Evelyn's diaries it was a familiar horticultural term by the time he used it.[20]

Increasingly, houses of the nobility were adapted to include space for 'exoticks'. The diarist Celia Fiennes (1642–1741) noted that at Woburn, home of the Dukes of Bedford, 'just by the dining room window is all sorts of pots of flowers and Curious greens, fine orange, Citron and Lemon trees and myrtles, striped filleroy and fine aloe plants'.[21]

Many of the newly discovered plants were thought to need protection, some all year round, as Celia Fiennes found on a visit to the Oxford Physic Garden – the first to be opened in England in 1621 and still going strong. She reports on a 'humble plant that grows on a slender stalk and do but strike it, it falls flat on the ground stalk and all, and after some time revives again and stands up, but these are nice plants and are kept mostly under glass, the air being too rough for them.' [22] Later she observed of the servants of New College, Oxford, that 'they take much delight in greens of all sorts, myrtle, orange and lemons and lorrestine growing in pots of earth, and so moved about from place to place and into the air sometimes.'[23]

The sixteenth and seventeenth centuries were the high points of orange growing in England. Evelyn claimed that the orange trees at Beddington had produced 10,000 oranges in one year. However, as continental travel improved in the eighteenth century, it no longer became essential to be able to produce home-grown fruit at such a high and labour-intensive cost, and orange trees fell out of favour as a plant to scent the home as well. Nevertheless, the British passion for bringing plants into the home was firmly established, with urban gardeners as keen as anyone to show off their horticultural skills.

CHAPTER 3

THE CHAMBER GARDEN

In 1722, the first book was published aimed not just at the urban gardener but specifically for those who lived 'in *London*, or other Cities, where much Sea-Coal is burnt . . . tho' they have never so little Room'. The lack of a garden in city homes was no longer such a hindrance to those who loved plants and flowers. Thomas Fairchild (1667–1729), author of *The City Gardener*, had seen 'the general Love my Fellow-Citizens have for Gardening . . . and of their furnishing their Rooms or Chambers with Basons of Flowers and Bough-pots, rather than not have something of a Garden before them'.[1]

One of the reasons for the increased interest in growing plants indoors was that the English home, particularly in cities and towns, was changing. By the end of the seventeenth century, England had undergone a massive social upheaval: a regicide, a civil war, a restored monarch and a plague. In spite of the devastation of the Great Fire in 1666, by 1700 London was a thriving city, with an ever-growing population of nearly 600,000 making it the largest city in Europe, closely followed by Paris.

Memories of the Fire of London were still vivid. Planning regulations brought in immediately afterwards meant that new houses were built of brick in preference to timber, an obvious fire hazard. The heavy wood panelling of the early seventeenth century was replaced with painted walls, which had the effect of bringing more light into the rooms.

Many people still had to collect their water from local wells or public water supplies known as 'conduits'. But increasingly wooden pipes were laid under the cobblestones. A few homes in London were able to connect to regular water supplies direct to a pump in their homes. However, this was an irregular service so there was still the need for tanks in which to store water. The lucky few had wells sunk in their gardens. Sophisticated and sometimes highly patterned, lead cisterns collected rainwater not just for the garden but also for the household. As a last resort, water could be bought from itinerant vendors.

Changes in building regulations introduced after the Fire of London stated that no floors or windows should extend outwards beyond the old property line. This was an old ruse that had led to roofs almost touching each other although there was the width of a street below. The immediate effect was to let more light into newly built city houses. The construction of windows also changed. Leading gave way to broad wooden bars, as classical rectangular panes became the norm. Homes were no longer restricted to the small leaded panels that had been so widely used during the Elizabethan and Jacobean eras.

The arrival in England of the sliding sash window from Holland with its sophisticated system of counterbalanced weights allowed much larger sheets of glass to be used. In spite of the Window Tax of 1696, which resulted in many householders blocking up windows in order to avoid paying it, the new style encouraged larger windows to be built and this brought more light into rooms. In addition, windowsills and balconies became a standard feature in house design. They were soon to be an important adjunct for floral displays. From 1708 it became the law to set windows at least four inches into the brickwork – a fire prevention measure that gave keen gardeners an outdoor sill on which to display pots and troughs.

The rebuilding work, especially in London, also had a marked effect on gardens as well. When the Swedish botanist Per Kalm visited London in the 1740s, he noted that:

At nearly every house in the town there was either in front towards the street, or inside the house and building, or in both, a little yard. They had commonly planted in these yards and round about them, partly in the earth and partly in pots and boxes, several of the trees, plants and flowers that can stand the coal-smoke in London. They thus sought to have some of the pleasant enjoyments of a country life in the midst of the hubbub of the town.[2]

Thomas Fairchild was keen for city gardeners to use the newly available space on balconies and windowsills for displaying plants. In addition to recommending bay, ivy and box, he suggested, among others, polyanthus, auriculas, wallflowers, double stocks, pinks and sweet Williams for outdoor potted displays. Myrtle and orange trees, Fairchild thought, did better indoors though he had seen some in pots outside houses in London – an early example of the city's microclimate perhaps. He had most enthusiasm for the aloe family. 'It is almost impossible to express all their Beauties,' he declared. 'I have now about thirty Sorts differing from one another.' Mr Smith, an apothecary he knew who lived in Aldermanbury in the City of London, had 'a very good Collection of these succulent or juicy Plants, which he has kept for many Years'.[3] Perhaps Mr Smith knew of the healing and soothing properties of the aloe's juice.

The aloe was one of the exciting varieties of plants brought into the country from the Near East, the New World and Southern Africa. Many of them were too tender to be grown outside all the year round, or looked so 'exotick' and different that they were grown for indoor display. For example, the crown imperial or 'Corona imperialis' (*Fritillaria imperialis*), which had arrived in Europe from Constantinople at the end of the sixteenth century, became extremely popular for indoor decoration in spite of its pungent smell.

Collectors such as Henry Compton, Bishop of London, introduced new plants from North America to his garden at Fulham Palace, and also through large nurseries such as the famous Brompton Park Nursery run by gardeners George London and Henry Wise. Compton also grew plants that were sent to him from South Africa via Holland such as *Pelargonium inquinans*. The first mention of a pelargonium flowering on British soil is found in Gerard's *Herball* of 1633 when he wrote of a plant he called *Geranium indicum noctu odoratum* 'as of late brought into this kingdom by the industry of Mr John Tradescant . . . I did see it in flower about the end of July, 1632, being the first time that it hath flowered with the owner thereof.' This later proved to be *P. triste*, so called because of its small, dark, 'sad' flowers. Gradually more plants arrived: *P. capitatum*, pink-flowered and with rose-scented leaves, was introduced in 1690 by Hans William Bentinck, William of Orange's head steward.

As the known world grew bigger, opportunities for plant hunting exploration burgeoned. Merchant sea captains kept collectors continually excited by what was brought home from America. Captain William Dampier managed to combine a spot of botanizing along with some piracy on his famed circumnavigations of the world and in 1699 discovered *Clianthus formosus* (Sturt's desert pea), later much grown in Victorian conservatories. In addition, individual explorers were finding and recording treasures never seen in Europe before.

Leading the way among passionate plant collectors was a woman whose horticultural legacy cannot be overestimated. Mary Capel Somerset, Duchess of Beaufort (d. 1715), came from an aristocratic family. Her father and two of her brothers all created substantial gardens in the South East of England. Mary's brother, Henry, gardened at Kew on what is now the site of the Royal Botanic Gardens, and here he raised many arrivals from the New World and beyond in his two greenhouses. These were still something of a novelty and restricted to members of the wealthy aristocracy or professional nurserymen.

Blessed with a generous income from her second marriage to the Duke of Beaufort, Mary Somerset was able to cultivate her gardens at Badminton, and at Beaufort House in London's Chelsea, just near the Chelsea Physic Garden, which had opened in 1673. By 1701, William Sherard, a botanist who had also been tutor to Mary's grandson, Henry, at Badminton, suggested that Mary's gardens were close to the best in Europe, 'being furnish'd with all conveniences imaginable, and a good stock of plants'.[4]

A good stock of plants indeed. The duchess kept meticulous records and her collection ran into thousands. Her great passion was for non-native plants and without doubt her meticulous care of the seeds that regularly arrived encouraged some of the greatest botanists in Europe to entrust her with their new finds from distant shores. She grew many in the conservatory which she had had built in the 1690s, and she called her 'infirmary'. Mary grew some of the earliest pelargonium arrivals in Britain. In 1701 she introduced *P. peltatum*, the first ivy-leafed geranium, now seen in a million window boxes every summer. As the landscape designer and author Stephen Switzer wrote in 1715, the 'Progress she made in Exotics' could not be matched by 'the Thousands' of those foreign Plants (by her as it were made familiar to this Clime) there regimented together, and kept in a wonderful deal of Health, Order and Decency'.[5] Almost the same sentiments were echoed three years later in Charles Evelyn's *The Lady's Recreation*. Appropriately, the duchess was later commemorated through the genus beaufortia, part of the myrtle family.

Mary was among the first in England to grow a *Hippeastrum puniceum* or Barbados lily. The assiduous gardener that she was, Mary noted its progress in detail.

. . . the description of the great Barbados Lylly given mee by Mr Doody [of the Chelsea Physic Garden in] 1691 the root much larger than any tulip root, the leaves have continue winter and summer from Aprill 1691: April 1693 being put into a hott bed it soone shot up a stalk for a flower and bore too flowers (upon one stalk) the later end of June the flowers are a delicate light scarlet the middle of each leafe of them a pure white, the chines are a blush colour with yellow seeds, the stalk was very large, 2 foot 3 inches high, 2 inches on[e] quarter in the compass, severall of the leaves are 2 foot one inch long, one of the lesser Lyllys roots blew the same flower.[6]

Although the duchess referred to all the great texts of the time such as Gerard and Parkinson, in her attempts to identify the botanical rarities sent to her, her frustration in these days of pre-Linnaean nomenclature is clear. She found trying to identify unknown seeds from the Far East the most exasperating, and wrote to physician and collector Sir Hans Sloane, with whom she corresponded regularly, that she wished there had been a painter on hand 'that would have better exprest this plant'.

> But finding it in no booke that I have, I hope it is a rarity, if it bee worth the keeping it is intended for you, it was rais'd from some East India seed without a name, it was sow'd I think 4 yeare past, has blowne twise, the eaves till neer there ful growth stand upright, but assoone as the stalk of the flower appears hang round the pot, but that I most wonder at is the root.[7]

Frustratingly, we will never know what this plant was! She was, however, successfully growing pelargoniums in 1700, including one 'from St Vincents' in the West Indies.

Given her comments on wanting visual records of her beloved plants, it is not surprising that in 1703, after she was widowed for the second time, Mary commissioned a Dutch artist called Everhard Kik or Kirk to produce an illustrated 'Flower Album' for her. The first volume was completed in 1705. Kik's student, a former Badminton footman named Daniel Frankcom, was sent to Kew to complete a second album. Whether the duchess brought these particular plants into her homes we cannot say for certain. But we do know from two sources that she did pioneer having a variety of plants on display in the living areas of her houses. There is a reference in her manuscripts to a 'Chrisanthemum in the drawing room window', and most clearly, in the comment by Thomas Fairchild in *The City Gardener*, published in 1722, seven years after the duchess's death: 'The Chimneys which are generally dress'd in Summer with fading Bough Pots, might be as well adorn'd at once with living Plants, as I have observ'd at her Grace's the late excellent Dutchess of *Beaufort*.'[8]

The bough, or beau, pots that Fairchild mentioned were large ceramic pots which sat in empty fireplaces during the summer months. Often decorated in the blue and white Delft style, they were designed to be filled with branches of shrubs. For a more lasting effect, Fairchild, among others, suggested filling them with flowering plants.

The West London nurserymen George London and Henry Wise sang the praises of *Campanula pyramidalis*, a biennial that had arrived in England near the end of the sixteenth century, in *The Retir'd Gard'ner*, published in 1706. 'The "Steeple-Bell-Flower", London and Wise wrote, 'will grow Six Foot high, all in a Pyramid of Blue Flowers, which will continue to Flower from the Time they begin to blow, 'till near Two or Three Months afterwards.'[9] With the campanula as a centrepiece, a pot of tuberose should be placed on either side, they suggested, with a pot of scarlet lychnis beside them, and two small pots of sweet basil and of 'Marum Syriacum' (*Origanum syriacum*) in front. Such was the popularity of *C. pyramidalis* for fireplace display that it became quickly known as the 'Chimney Bellflower'.

Thomas Fairchild, a portly but jolly man, had established a nursery in Hoxton in 1691. This was a popular area for nurserymen, who were possibly attracted by the local clay works easily able to supply their pot needs. An outstanding botanist, he is justly famous for producing the first hybrid, Fairchild's Mule Pink, in 1717, *Dianthus caryophyllus* x *barbatus*, a cross between a carnation and a sweet William. Writing on the different techniques needed to be used by town gardens with limited space for displaying plants, Fairchildsuggests that 'the Chambers of a House may have their Ornaments, which may last well for a considerable Time, especially while Fires are not in use.'[10] He was full of grand ideas to match those he had seen in Mary Somerset's homes.

If one was to have a Pyramid of Shelves to be covered with Pots of blossoming Orange-Trees, with Fruit upon them, intermixt with Mirtles, Aloes, *&c.* for Variety-sake, it would be extremely beautiful for the Summer; and the Pots, to add the greater Beauty, might be of Delph Ware, or well painted, to stand in Dishes, which are now in Use; so that when we water the Plants, the Water will not run upon the Floor.[11]

Fairchild's enthusiasm for bringing plants indoors was tempered with the knowledge that they would need careful treatment if they were to last.

Box or Privet to be train'd up in a Fan Fashion, will do very well in Chimneys for a Summer, if they are now and then set abroad at Night, and in Showers of Rain, and are regularly water'd' and with these we may also place white Lillies taken up in Bunches, just as they are coming into Flowers, and potted they will make a good Show, and will last beautiful a long Time, and perfume the House almost as well as a Tuberose . . . To further this Variety, if we have Convenience of a Place to set Pots abroad, or without, Doors, we may have most of the Annual Flowers to interchange from Time to Time, as it may be judg'd proper.[12]

In the often harsh English winter, tender plants needed protection. Space was also needed to 'bring on' flowers for home decoration. As glass became cheaper, many in the wealthy classes constructed a separate 'glass' house to overwinter plants. In addition to the sun's rays warming the air around the plants, iron stoves were also brought in to increase temperatures. Charcoal was burned to avoid the noxious fumes that coal fires gave off. These 'stove houses' rarely had glass roofs since it was thought that heat rather than light was important for the plants' survival.

A less expensive option was to keep hardy plants in a hotbed to encourage early flowering. This was an excavated pit that was then filled with fresh manure, which released its heat to the plants above. These beds were usually situated against a wall. Some form of protection was rigged up in the form of a wooden frame over which canvas matting could be fixed. Only the grandest of houses could afford the stove houses and hotbeds necessary to produce freshly cut flowers for elaborate flower arrangements throughout the year.

Lesser households relied on growing hardy plants in pots outside and then bringing them indoors when required. There was no shortage of written advice on which plants would be suitable for this treatment. There are three main contemporary sources that, combined, produce a list of just over 200 different types of plants thought suitable for displaying indoors in the early eighteenth century. The earliest list comes from Leonard Meager's book, *The English Gardener*, published in 1688. Meager, a gardener in Northamptonshire before he joined the famous West London nursery, Brompton Park, run by George London and Henry Wise, had several categories of suggested plants including 'A catalogue of Flowers, both such as are yearly to be raised of seed, and others of divers kinds, for the furnishing of Flowerpots, and adorning the rooms of Houses'. Meager claimed that 'many are very much taken and affected with furnishing of their flower-pots, for the adorning of some Rooms in their Houses &c.'[13]

The second list comes from John Evelyn's translation of the standard work of Jean de La Quintinie, kitchen gardener to Louis XIV, published in England as *The Compleat Gard'ner* in 1693. Since the term 'flower-pot' was interchangeable with what we would now call a vase, some of both Meager and de La Quintinie's suggestions may well have been for cut flower arrangements rather than potted flowering plants.

There is no doubt, however, that the plants listed in the third book, Batty Langley's *New Principles of Gardening* (1728), are definitely for flowerpots not flower vases. Langley makes this clear in the beginning of his section on the 'Rules for the Adorning the Chimneys of Halls, Chambers, &c. with such fragrant Flowers as are most suitable, *viz.* Truly Innocent, Beautiful, and Pleasant'.[14]

In Order to truly execute this Work in the Best Manner, we must, first, be furnished with beautiful Flower-Pots of *Dutch* Ware, *China, &c.* wherein other Garden Flower-Pots must be placed, in which our Flowers are to grow.[15]

Here is the first mention of ceramic decorated pots used as 'cache-pots', that is to literally hide pots, the common or garden terracotta pots that the plants would have been grown in outside. Langley explains how he thinks they should be planted up.

First then, to begin the Year, prepare some indifferent good Mold, with which to fill as many Pots as are sufficient for your Chimney; and in the Middle of each Pot, plant a very large Root, or two, of Snow-Drops, of the double Kind, which environ with a Circle of the several Sorts of Crocus. This Work being done at the Time when Snow-Drops and Crocus have done Blowing, will, in the *January* following, make a glorious Appearance, and grace their Places of Abode, wherein they then are placed.[16]

For February Langley suggested polyanthus, hyacinths and violets, 'all which being planted in the like Manner, will succeed the preceding, and be very entertaining'. Hyacinths and violets are also recommended for March, to which Langley suggests adding 'Stock-July-Flowers' planted in the middle of one pot where 'they will make a very beautiful Appearance, and their sweet Odors be very agreeable'.

When it comes to April, there is more choice and in addition to the hyacinths, Langley adds wallflowers, tulips, ranunculus, anemones, jonquils, narcissi and auriculas, all popular with florists, keen amateur growers.

In the Center of some Pots plant a Wall-Flower; in others, a Cluster of Tulips, or Jonquils, because they both grow indifferent high; and in Order to have them in the Greatest Beauty, let every Tulip in each Pot be of a different Colour; and that they may make their best Appearance, place a handsome Flower-Stick in the Center of each Pot, with a gilt Head, to which tie up every Flower with Thread, &c. but in a free loose Manner, so as not to present a stiff Bundle of Flowers, void of Freedom, in which the Beauty of every Thing consists. The Jonquils must be encompassed with a Circle of Ranunculus; the Tulips, with a Circle of Hyacinths; the Stock-July-Flowers, with Anemonies; and the Wall-Flowers with Narcissus.[17]

Langley was an enthusiastic user of bulbous flowers for indoor growing, though his rainbow choice of tulip colours together with the gilded flower support might seem rather garish to modern tastes. But they were the favourite plant to grow indoors, particularly when it was discovered that they could grow in water.

Among Langley's other suggestions are two types of apple tree (*Malus* 'Calville Rouge d'été' and *M.* 'Calville Blanche d'été'), 'Sweet-Brier' (*Rosa rubiginosa*), 'White Jessemine' *(Jasminum officinale)* and 'Honey-Suckles'. All these, he recommended, were to be grown 'round-headed' or as standards, the easier to be transported into the house where either the fruit or the scent could be appreciated.

Auriculas, one of Langley's favourite indoor plants, had first appeared in England in the late sixteenth century, possibly brought by the Huguenots. Middleton and Rochdale in Lancashire, where many Flemish weavers settled, soon became centres for auricula growing. Gerard described them accurately in 1597, claiming that they 'do grow in our London gardens' in spite of coming from 'the Alpish and Helvetian mountains'. John Parkinson also praised them since 'they are not unfurnished with a pretty sweete sent, which doth add an encrease of pleasure in those that make them an ornament for their wearing.'[18]

Although auriculas are hardy, they have long been grown in pots for display, a fashion that is currently going through something of a revival. By the late seventeenth century, auriculas had joined the carnation, tulip, anemone and ranunculus as a show flower for florists. The earliest known meeting or 'Florist Feast' to show off and discuss their chosen plants was in Norwich in 1631. Carnations or gillyflowers were frequently grown in pots, as were the other florists' flowers, as they had to be portable even if they were grown outside. All these plants were now firmly established as essential decoration for all but the humblest homes.

CHAPTER 4

THE FASHION FOR FORCING

In the hundred years since Sir Hugh Platt had written about gardening 'within doores', plant growing for the home had changed dramatically. Across the country, many wealthy households now had hothouses for growing the exotic plants that were arriving regularly from across the world. New methods of forcing plants into flower in winter and early spring meant that it was possible to have flowering plants in the home virtually the whole year round.

By the start of the eighteenth century plants were readily available through reputable nurseries such as those belonging to Robert Furber or George London and Henry Wise at Brompton Park, which was the biggest in the capital. London and Wise stocked around 40,000 plants including many 'greens' and exotic tender plants such as the ever-popular citrus, jasmines, bays and myrtles.

On the other side of the City, in Hoxton, nurseryman John Cowell competed with his neighbour Fairchild and specialized in succulents, especially agaves and aloes. He was also one of the first to open his garden to the public and built a display house to show off his collections, which the public could visit for a fee. Not surprisingly, his gardening publication was called *The Curious and Profitable Gardener* (1730).

Pelargoniums were also becoming popular. In the 1730s, William Sherard's brother James was growing half a dozen varieties of 'geraniums' at his garden in Eltham, and by 1753 Linnaeus had described twenty-five known varieties. Around this time, Philip Miller cultivated *P. betulinum*, which was to become a parent of the modern Regal strain, as was *P. cululatum*, another Bentick introduction. In 1787, French botanist L'Heritier reclassified the Cape geraniums as pelargoniums though over two centuries later they are still frequently misnamed.

Auriculas were regularly displayed at florists' spring festivals. A report from a newspaper on 16 April 1729 shows how popular they were.

On Tuesday last a great Feast of Gardiners call'd Florists was held in the Dog in Richmond Hill, at which were present about 130 in

Number; after Dinner several shew'd their Flowers (most of them Auricula's) and five ancient and judicious Gardiners were Judges to determine whose flowers excelled . . . a Gardiner of Barnes in Surrey was so well furnished with good Flowers, that the Judge in the affair, ordered him two Spoons and one Ladle.[1]

Around this time, a 'break' produced varieties with startling new colours, edging and a white meal known to growers as 'paste'. Although auriculas are hardy, these fancy varieties needed protecting from the weather if they were not to spoil when in flower. Keen growers displayed their precious show plants when in flower in 'theatres', outdoor shelved staging with a roof.

A good deal of swapping went on between keen growers but one of the perils of being a 'city' gardener, according to Fairchild, was that one had little contact with country-trained nurserymen who knew what they were selling. Produce markets in London sold plants as a sideline but this was something that Fairchild cautioned keen town gardeners against buying there.

For most of those People who sell the Trees and Plants in *Stocks* and other Markets, are Fruiterers, who understand no more of Gardening than a Gardener does the making up the Compound Medicines of an Apothecary. They often tell us the Plants will prosper, when there is no Reason of Hopes of their growing at all; for I and others have seen Plants that were to be sold in the Markets, that were as uncertain of Growth as a Piece of *Noah's* Ark would be, had we it here to plant; but when such Plants are bought at the Gardens where they were raised, there can be no Deceit, without the Gardener who sold them loses his Character.[2]

It was the appropriately named botanist and physician Nehemiah Grew who saw, in 1682, that hyacinths and tulips could be 'forced' to flower in the winter by keeping the plants warm. Fifty years later a Swedish scientist called Samuel Treiwald wrote an article for the Royal Society of London: 'An Account of Tulips and other Bulbous Plants, flowering much sooner, when their Bulbs are placed on Bottles filled with Water, than when planted in the Ground'. Treiwald claimed the bulbs he had set on glasses filled only with water bloomed five months earlier than they would have done in the ground.

In the same journal, Philip Miller (1692–1771), curator of the Chelsea Physic Garden and author of *The Gardener's Dictionary* (1724), which ran to eight editions in his own lifetime, reported on his own experiments with Treiwald's methods. Miller found that by placing bulbs on plain glass carafes almost filled with 'common Thames water' and keeping them in the greenhouse over winter, the hyacinths bloomed six weeks before the tulips and narcissi and thus he was able to recommend it as 'an amusement for display in the chambers of those without a garden'.

At the beginning of the eighteenth century, hyacinths were the most highly prized bulb for forcing into flower and bringing into the house. According to Philip Miller, in 100 years the number of varieties had jumped from just four blue and white varieties to a staggering 2,000. A great part of this popularity was due to the breeding of double and triple hyacinths by Pieter Voerhelm, a Dutch grower. At first Voerhelm had thrown away the doubles as they appeared, thinking them worthless. One winter, debilitated by illness, he found one he had missed which rather took his fancy. The third variation propagated from that bulb he called 'King of Great Britain', after King William. It made him a rich man, selling in 1760 for the staggering amount of £100 a bulb. Through the process of hybridization, the stem of the plant had shrunk and the 'bells' of the flower compacted to make a highly scented flower head as opposed to the loose, leggy wild version.

Holland remained the centre for bulb growing and sales to Britain were buoyant. In 1776, Robert Edmeades, who ran a seed and gardening business in the heart of the City of London, at No. 11 Fish Street Hill near the Monument, produced a catalogue listing over 1,200 varieties of hyacinths. 'Goldmine', which came in red, purple and scarlet, was aptly named since it cost £15 a bulb. The elusive supposedly black 'Flora nigra' cost even more at £21. Bizarrely there was a double flesh-coloured variety which was named after Admiral Byng, who had been court-martialled and shot for his failure to relieve the island of Minorca from the French.

Such was the popularity of hyacinths in the eighteenth century that china manufacturers quickly responded with suitable containers for high-class drawing rooms. Mrs Philip Lybbe Powys wrote in her diary in 1767, after a visit to Queen Charlotte's apartments, that every room was filled with 'roses, carnations and hyacinths, &c., dispersed in the prettiest manner imaginable in jars and different flower-pots on stands'.[3] After Lord Harcourt gave Mrs Delany a yellow variety, 'Ophir', in 1780, she used it as one of the few cultivars that she named in her tissue paper mosaic pictures. The hyacinth was the only florists' flower to be mentioned by Jane Austen in *Northanger Abbey*. Catherine Morland spied them in a shop window and quickly 'learnt to love [them]'.

In 1734, nurseryman Robert Furber (1688–1756) added a new chapter to his book *The Flower Garden Display'd*, published in 1732. It was entitled, 'A Flower-Garden for Gentlemen and Ladies: or The Art of raising Flowers without any Trouble; to blow in full Perfection in the Depth of Winter, in a Bed-Chamber, Closet, or Dining Room'. This 'art' was, the chapter claimed, 'as practised by Sir Thom[as] More, Bart'. There are no records of who this particular Thomas More was and he is not listed as a baronet of this time. However, there are mentions of a Thomas More as a botanist and since Furber did not claim authorship of the chapter, we can assume that the enthusiastic words that follow were penned by More himself. Readers learned how 'to raise many Sorts of Flowers in a Chamber, in the greatest Smoke of *London*, and in the midst of Winter; and to have them blow in full Perfection within the Twelve Days of *Christmas*, as I had my self in the last *Christmas* past'.[4]

In the small, close-knit world of London gardeners, botanists and nurserymen in the early eighteenth century, it is not surprising that More and Furber knew about Miller's experiments. Not only was Furber's nursery at Kensington Gore, less than a mile away from the Chelsea Physic Garden, but also his son William was apprenticed to Miller for a premium of £4 in 1722. Furber was popular in genteel society, and through his skill as a nurseryman, his Kensington Nursery soon became a fashionable shopping spot for the likes of floral artist Mrs Delany and her sister. Word-of-mouth recommendation was important to nurserymen at a time when press advertising in general was minimal. Furber was also the first nurseryman to produce book-form catalogues at a time when only seedsmen advertised in newspapers.

Thomas More left detailed descriptions of how he grew a variety of spring-flowering bulbs including daffodils, jonquils, narcissi, tulips and hyacinths. To grow them in, he had bought 'some Dozens of Flint Tumbler-Glasses of the *Germans* who Cut them prettily and sell them Cheap . . . whole Pints to Halves and Quarters. These Glasses [were] wide at the top and tapering to the Bottom.' Bearing in mind Philip Miller's instructions, he 'took particular care that no water shou'd be fill'd up to wet any more than just the Bottoms of the Bulbous Roots, for that would certainly rot them and have destroy'd all my Hopes'.[5]

In addition to More's experiments with growing individual bulbs in glass vases, he also wrote about his experiments with growing plants and bulbs to flower indoors throughout the winter. To start with, he ordered four large clay flowerpots from 'the Red-ware Pot-house'. He insisted that they were made from 'true season'd Pot-earth, that the Frost might not scale them' in case he did ever want to use them outside during the winter. The pots were 17¾ inches (45 cm) in diameter and 11¾ inches (30 cm deep) and were designed to sit in metal stands comprised of a ring on legs, which held the pot and allowed it to be easily lifted in and out. More had the pots painted to look like imitation blue and white Delftware.

More's recipe for these pots was as follows: a crown imperial (*Fritillaria imperialis*) was placed in the middle, surrounded by tulips of unknown colours, which were, in turn, ringed with double white and blue hyacinths. Tucked between the hyacinths were anemones, encircled by white and yellow polyanthus narcissus, then a ring of large double daffodils, a ring of mixed crocus, and lastly, a ring of double snowdrops. On two sides were two hepatica and, on the opposite sides, two fritillaria, possibly *F. meleagris*. At the end of September, More placed two of the pots 'without my Chamber Window, in the Passage against the Steeple of St *Brides* Church'.[6] The other two pots he placed in the metal ring supports inside on an easterly facing windowsill. These he watered with rainwater he had saved, 'or else with *Thames* water'.

The experiment was a great success and More was eager to pass on his experiences to others.

> Before *Twelfth Day* [6 January] I had some *Crocus* blown in my Chamber, and *Snowdrops* blowing in as full Perfection as in a Country Garden. When the *Crocus* ad done blowing within, the next that follow'd was the double *Daffs*, which blow'd full as fair both in Size and Colour; the *Anemonys* shot out tall Flowers, but were crouded too much, and I believe would have done very well in single Basons with more Room; after these came the *Polyanthus Narcissus* in all Perfection, as did the several colour'd double *Hyacinths*, and most agreeably perfum'd my Chamber, lasting in Bloom till the middle of *March*: The *Crown Imperial* was by that Time grown about two Foot and a half high, with Flower Buds at the Top.[7]

In addition to the two large pots, More also had 'several *Crocus's* that gave me their Bloom with full Strength in little China Tea-pots I ranged close to the Glass in my Chamber Window'.[8] At a time when not only pieces of china but also the tea itself were highly prized, one can only wonder at what More's wife, if he had one, must have thought of her precious wares used in this way.

How did More's other pots that had languished in the shadow of St Brides suffering 'all the Inclemency of this last Winter' fare? The crocuses did not start flowering until the end of February, and the snowdrops just after in early March. The daffodils and hyacinths followed 'all in great Perfection', together with the crown imperials. By the end of March, the *Narcissi polyanthus* were in flower. The hepaticas had flowered as well inside as outside as did the fritillaries, but the tulips had not been a great success although some had flower. More put this down to overcrowding.

More was spurred on by the success he had had the previous summer with bowls of flowering annuals raised especially in his hotbeds for his new indoor pots. He had grown double African marigolds, marvel of Peru (*Mirabilis jalapa*), capsicum, cockscomb, amaranthus, orange mint and other unnamed variegated herbs, all of which had thrived. '[They] went thro' their Bloom within the Chamber and without,' More reported, 'the *Capsicums* changing to their fine Red, and continuing with me till the approach of Winter, when I displaced them to begin my aforesaid Trail on the Spring Flowers.'[9]

Having managed to bring all these plants into bloom 'in a Room without the Help of the Sun's enlivening Heat, or the refreshing Dews, or the more clarified Air, but only by a due and proper Watering' set More on a path to do yet more experiments with his plants indoors. In what may seem to us a very obvious statement, More decided that what prompted plants to grow was water. Plants would not flourish in dry soil; therefore, he postulated, it might surely be possible to grow plants just in water. This early experiment in hydroponics might have the added benefit, he added, of appealing to 'the Curious of the Fair Sex', because it would be a 'much neater and cleanlier Way' of growing flowers 'with the most delicious Perfumes thereof, in their Chambers or Parlours'. This led More to do his own experiments, similar to both Treiwald's and Philip Miller's, with growing bulbs only in water.

More had realized that straight-sided glasses would be of no use since the bulbs would slip too easily into the water. So, in addition to the glass tumblers he had bought, he also bought some large glass 'basons' or bowls that tapered from top to bottom. Ingeniously he then cut sheets of cork, just over a centimetre thick, to fit into the tops of the bowls or the glasses with holes cut out in them proportionate to the side of the bulb, or 'roots' as More called them, to stop them slipping too far into the water and rotting. This also allowed him to grow more than one size of bulb in the same bowl. In some glasses, he grew one bulb only, some two, and in others three or four. In the cork for the bowls, he cut several smaller holes allowing him to grow several bulbs 'which might blow together with the more Splendor'.

The experiment was a great success. Having planted up his glasses and bowls with a variety of narcissus, several sorts of hyacinth, tulip, crocus, daffodil and jonquil, he topped them up with '*Thames* Water [being] the best, as being strongly impregnated with prolific Matter, like rich Earth well manur'd for Corn or Garden Uses', so that it just touched the bottoms of bulbs.[10] They were placed on his windowsills. More was then faced with a problem that any keen windowsill gardener will recognize – he could then not open his casement windows with ease – and he was worried that if he did try and open them, the bowls might fall out!

Within a few days, the white fibrous roots started to appear and, as every child who has tried growing a hyacinth in water will remember, More found this 'a most diverting Pleasure to behold'. He regularly topped up the water in the containers, changing it once a week since he thought that the plants were drawing nutrients from the water and would exhaust its fertility. In this way, he had polyanthus narcissus in flower before Christmas from a late September start, followed shortly after by several hyacinths and crocus. The Persian iris (*Iris persica*), he treated differently, lifting them from the ground seven days before Christmas when they had just started showing some green growth, and transferring them to one of his glass containers. Within days, they were flowering, much to the amazement of his gardener.

This all happened, More was convinced, because there were constant fires in his room during the day and evening, although they were allowed to go out at night. His flowers did not fail 'either for want of Sun, Air, Dew, or Rain, and in the Smoke of the Town in the worst of Weather, nor in the Smoke of the Room by a Fault in the Chimney, which as so great, that sometimes they were hardly to be seen for the Smoke'. This would allow the 'curious Ladies' to be supplied with 'most agreeable Perfumes for their Chambers, Parlours, &c. and with Nosegays to adorn their Bosom at *Christmas* . . . at a time when the Gardens are divested of all their Beauty'.[11]

More reassured his readers that this new process of growing flowering bulbs indoors would not kill them. By planting them in the garden 'as soon as they have done blowing', they would recover and flower again outside the following spring. In addition, he claimed, 'all Fibrous Roots will grow and blow' if grown in water.

> It is much better for their lasting in Bloom than putting cut Flowers in Flower-pots, which usually decay in four or five Days, when these on the Glasses will keep blowing for a Month. I have had all this *Christmas* great *Double Daisies*, red and white *Primroses*, and strip'd *Polyanthus* in full fair, and sweet Blooms, flourishing upon my Glasses in as much Perfection as they would have done in the Garden in Summer, and by this means the Chamber Garden may be continued all the Year round.[12]

Finally, More writes probably the earliest description of a method of growing a version of 'cut and come again' salad greens on the windowsill, perfect, he says, to supply a small family with 'sallets'. Using his cork and glass bowl method once again, More pierced the cork 'very full of small Holes', topped up the basin with Thames water until the cork was soaked with it, and then covered the cork with a thick mix of 'all the Sorts of young Sallet Seed which you like best'. Placed on a warm windowsill, within a few days the seeds sprouted and were 'fit for pulling'. The benefits to the new band of urban dwellers were easy to see.

> What a pleasant Diversion must this give as well as save much Charge; there will be no need of the Expence of a Gardener, nor the making Hot-beds, nor the Carpenter's Work for Frames, nor the Glazier's for Lights to these Frames, nor the Attendance on them with Mats, &c. only a few Basons, a little Cork, and good *Thames Water,* with the Garden Sallet Seed, all but an inconsiderable Charge to give the Lady or Gentleman an agreeable Amusement with very little Trouble in the Windows of their Chambers, Parlours, or any other warm Rooms.[13]

If only indoor gardening was always that easy. But for those eighteenth-century gardeners with green fingers, this was a new dawn of plant growing. In an era that was full of a thirst for scientific knowledge, curiosity about how plants grow brought a sense of control within reach of all. In addition, the burgeoning commercialism of interior design was to alter the way plants were displayed in the home forever. As London and Wise noted in the *Retir'd Gard'ner,* 'the pots in which we plant our Tuberoses, are an Ornament properer for Windows than Parterres.'[14] Plant containers were no longer just made from red clay but were becoming more refined as suited the sophisticated mid-eighteenth-century interior.

CHAPTER 5

'PORCOIPINS FOR SNOWDRIPS'

E stimates vary but between 5,000 to 10,000 different species of plants were introduced into Britain in the eighteenth century. Botany was becoming not just an amateur interest but also a life-long passion for many. Links with the New World tightened with the friendship of John Bartram in America and Quaker Peter Collinson in London. From his garden outside Philadelphia, Bartram was responsible for sending countless seeds in what were known as 'Bartram's boxes' back to England, which were distributed by Collinson to botanical gardens and keen growers across Europe. Collinson also sent them to Carl Linnaeus (1707–78) so that he could name the finds according to his new simplified system of nomenclature. This was based on a hierarchical scheme of families, genera and species.

Another major figure in eighteenth-century horticultural history was Sir Joseph Banks, later honorary director of the Royal Botanic Gardens at Kew. He had become a passionate botanist while at Oxford and joined Captain Cook's first voyage to the South Pacific in 1768. Fellow voyagers on Cook's second trip were Johann Forster and his son also called Johann, who discovered many plants in South America and the South Sea islands. Also in that party was Francis Masson, a Scotsman, who was responsible for sending back over 500 plants from the Cape area, including the soon to be enormously popular Cape heathers and pelargoniums, and, from the Canary Isles, forms of cineraria. Francis Masson (1741–1806) was contracted by the Royal Botanic Gardens at Kew. Among his discoveries were *P. cordifolium, P. echinatum, P. grandiflorum* (the sweetheart pelargonium), *P. panduriforme, P. reniforme* and *P. tomentosum*.

In spite of the wealth of new plant material arriving in Britain, flowers were banished to the kitchen plot, and gardens were increasing landscaped in the style of Lancelot 'Capability' Brown (1716–83). They did not vanish from the home: they could be seen on wallpaper, clocks, carpets, fire screens, even inlays on furniture, and on furnishing and clothing fabrics. Mrs Delany's court dress was covered with over 200 different flowers she had embroidered herself. Most court dresses would have been made of Spitalfields silk decorated with exquisitely accurate depictions of flowers such as those by famed designer Anna Maria Garthwaite (1690–1763). Similarly, a large tapestry wall hanging done by Anne Grant of Monymusk in Scotland and dated 1750 shows a flower-strewn room with roses and honeysuckle twining round pillars, vases of cut flowers and, right in the middle, a large potted flowering tree.

Expanding cities brought with them a new sort of commercialism aimed at homeowners. Silks and carpets, china and clocks were now on sale in most city centres or, failing that, to order. While the poor still lived in rented rooms with shared facilities, the wealthier middling sorts were able to either rent or buy one of the newly built terraced houses in England's larger towns and cities. Designed in a style still popular with families, these houses often had full-length first floor windows giving out on to small balconies. Windows had deeper sills for fire protection and at street level, entrance steps lead up to front doors with half-moon fan-lights above them.

Floral motifs continued to be a part of interior decorating prompted by the influx and availability of cheaper furnishing items from the Far East. The introduction of mahogany from the West Indies brought changes in furniture design. Initially mahogany was cheap to import and easier to shape and polish to a high shine finish than oak. A rush of smaller purpose-built items of furniture such as writing desks and card tables appeared on the market. Most furniture was designed to be compact and portable, one of the reasons why eighteenth-century furniture has remained so popular. Chippendale, for example, popularized the 'tripod' table, a circular table with a top that tipped vertically for storage against a wall.

The centre of most reception or drawing rooms was kept clear with pieces of furniture such as chairs and tea tables placed around the walls of the room and brought out when needed. Even in the dining rooms, spare chairs would be stored against the walls, allowing the table to be used easily for other occupations such as sewing or writing during the day. Only in the back parlour or library would larger pieces such as bureaus or desk cabinets remain in place. Mrs Delany, whose exquisite 'paper mosaicks' of flowers brought her a close friendship with the royal family, described what furniture moving was involved when she was visited by Princess Amelia.

All the most comfortable sophas and great chairs, all the pyramids of books (adorning *almost every chair*), all the tables and *even the spinning wheel* were banish'd for that day, and the blew damask chairs set in prim form around the room.[1]

Newly built homes had a light feel to them. Panelling was no longer needed to give air ventilation against damp. It was replaced by plaster and decorated with wallpapers from China. Mirrors were extremely popular especially since the window tax at the end of the seventeenth century had induced many householders to brick up some side windows. Not only did the mirrors reflect light but also the newly fashionable china *garniture de chemineés* sets of lidded jars and vases displayed on mantelpieces.

Although water for most rooms of the house still had to be carried upstairs, many new houses had piped water into the kitchen. This surprisingly sophisticated system allowed families access to water not just for their houses but for their gardens, as explained by visiting Franco-American writer Louis Simond in 1810:

> June 6. – There has not been a drop of rain for the last six weeks; the verdure of the town gardens is destroyed, and the streets are very dusty, except the genteelest ones, which are inundated twice a-day by means of carts and fire-plugs communicating with the pipes under-ground, which circulate throughout the town.[2]

Another technological benefit was that for the first time in Britain there was widespread commercial production of decorative pots in which to display plants. Ornamental clay flowerpots were available in England certainly in medieval times but these were designed for outdoor use. Imports from Holland were available in the seventeenth century but it was not until the early eighteenth century that there was any large-scale production of designs suitable for indoors.

The greatest influence on horticultural ceramics for the home in the eighteenth century was also one of the century's best-known designers and manufacturers of chinaware, Josiah Wedgwood. The first potter to mark his earthenware and use his own name for his factory, we tend to think of Wedgwood only in terms of dinner services and small ornamental pieces. But in the early days of his business, plant pots were an important part of his sales list, reflecting Wedgwood's talent for homing in on the latest popular activity where there was a possibility of increased business.

When, in 1774, his friend and partner Thomas Bentley opened their London showroom in the fashionable Soho area of London's West End, there was a dedicated 'Flowerpot Room' to display their 'Root flowerpots of various sorts, ornamented and plain. Essence pots, Bough pots, and Cornucopias'. After a visit to the showroom, Mrs Delany described feeling 'quite giddy at looking at so much crockery ware'.[3]

Bough pots were still the most popular way of displaying plants indoors, filling empty fireplaces during the summer months. The ever practical Wedgwood noted down in his commonplace book his requisites for the essential properties of a bough pot: 'To stand firm, but not look heavy ... To hold a good quantity of flowers ... To be of a different earth, colour, or composition, from the common earthenware in use at the time being and To come at a moderate price.'[4]

Always the consummate businessman, Wedgwood continued to list his thoughts on sizing and the ever-widening market for these pots: 'Any beautiful form may be adopted, with the above properties some to form pyramids, some finished with a sloping cover, some large for hearths, under slabs, &c. – others less, and of vase forms, for chimney pieces – and some cheap for windows in common houses.'[5]

Wedgwood wisely listened to his clients, especially his female ones, as well as absorbing their changing tastes into his designs. In 1772, he told Bentley of a visit he had had from Mr & Mrs Southwell at Etruria, friends whose opinions he respected since 'they are both adepts in these matters'. Together they examined all his designs, measuring them against his list of principles and found that those that were not selling, not surprisingly, did not match up to his set of standards. To his delight, the Southwells approved of his new 'bow' pots. 'I now have much clearer ideas of bow pots &c than before & believe I can make them to <u>please your customers</u>,' he wrote with enthusiasm.[6]

This enthusiasm was also directed at Mrs Southwell, who, having 'examin'd every flowerpot', clearly was a tremendous hit with Josiah. 'Mrs Southwell is a Charming Woman. I am more & more in love with her every time I see her & having such a Mistress in the Science of flower dressing, I hope our future productions will shew that I have profited accordingly.'[7] This is the only tantalizing glimpse we have of the woman who excited Wedgwood so much. But knowing that Josiah was not only a happily married man, but also a natural-born entrepreneur and businessman, it is refreshing to think that it was Mrs Southwell's opinions that excited him more than her dimples or ringlets.

Wedgwood's enthusiasm had run away with him, however, and within ten days of Mrs Southwell's visit, the factory was 'over head & ears' in bough pots.[8] With anything to do with plants and flowers, timing is everything and Wedgwood had gone into full production at the wrong time of year.

The bowpots we are now making every body admires, & I am pretty certain they are right, but, we seem as unfortunate in timeing this article as in opening our rooms in Bath. – However they will be ready for spring, & indeed our customers must by them in London in the Winter to take them into the Country in the Spring.[9]

Wedgwood was always keen to promote the breadth of his stock. When it came to plant holders, this was no exception and there was something for every pocket:

Of *root pots*, as well for bulbous as other roots, and of *flower pots* or *bouquetiers*, there is a great variety, both in respect to pattern and colour, and the prices vary accordingly. The flower and root pots are from sixpence a piece, to seven shillings and sixpence. Some of the bulbous-root pots are finished higher, with bas-reliefs, enamelling, &c, and the prices are in proportion. The ornamental or case flower pots are from one shilling to eighteen shillings or more.[10]

The root pots were designed for holding either bulbs or plants and could be ordered with matching patterns to flowerpots for holding cut flowers. These were not vases with narrow necks (which Wedgwood also produced) but cleverly designed pots with removable lids designed to be dual purpose: pierced lids for supporting flower stems and cupped lids for holding bulbs. It was a practical idea which must have been appreciated by many a housemaid. He suggested this so 'that the flowers may be taken off all together with the cover, to change the water, which soon grows putrid'.[11]

This made for confusion even among those who worked for Wedgwood himself. Wedgwood's representative in Liverpool in 1767, Mr Bentley, received a letter from Josiah, explaining that he had been mistaken about the use of one of the items sent to him from the Etruria factory. 'Your punch bowl is a Winter flowerpot, not to be fill'd with water, & branches of flowers, but with sand, & bulbous roots & is to those baubles made in Glass for growing one bulbous root, what a Garden is to a flowerpot.'[12] Wedgwood's disdain for the single hyacinth glass was clear.

Wedgwood was also producing 'potpouries' for the home, jars to hold scented confections decorated to match his other china items if required, with a lid that could be removed when the room was occupied. Although roses remained the most popular ingredient for pot pourri, lemon verbena (*Aloysia triphylla*) arrived in Britain via Spain in the eighteenth century and quickly became a vital ingredient as flavouring for scented mixtures and jellies and cakes. As with so many strongly scented plants, the flowers of lemon verbena are insignificant but when crushed the leaves are one of horticulture's great surprises.

Another scented plant to have recently arrived in England was the heliotrope, *Heliotropium peruvianum*. 'Cherry Pie' as it was to become known, though it smells nothing like cherries, was discovered in Peru in 1735 by French botanist Joseph de Jussieu. By the time it arrived in England in 1757, via the Chelsea Physic Garden, it was highly prized for its intoxicating scent, and in France 'no vase was thought too precious or too costly to contain it'.[13] Ten years later, Lady Mary Campbell Coke was given a present of 'a pot of heliotropium odoratisimum' which, she was told, 'will do as well in my room as in a green-house; 'tis a delightful smell'.[14]

While it would take a hundred years for heliotrope to reach its peak of popularity, the most popular plant to have indoors during the eighteenth and early nineteenth centuries was mignonette (*Reseda odorata*), known as 'Frenchman's Darling'. Under its common name, mignonette, reseda crops up time and time again and, in the days of relaxed spelling rules, in a variety of different versions: mignionette, mignoinet, mignoinette, all of which stem from the French translation, 'Little Darling', far prettier than the English 'Fragrant Weed'. It is easy to see how it got that name, however, since there is nothing striking about the little flower, which in horticulture language is usually called 'insignificant'. What was significant, however, is the plant's delicious scent at a time when it was still important to perfume rooms and mask odours from the outside streets.

An ancient plant that has been found in Egyptian tombs, legend has it that mignonette was first grown in England in 1742 at the garden of Richard Bateman's Grove House in Old Windsor, having been sent there via Paris from North Africa. The Chelsea Physic Garden acquired seed from Dr Adrian van Royen, Professor of Botany at Leyden Botanic Garden, ten years later. Philip Miller described the plant as smelling of raspberries and it was soon scenting every fashionable drawing room and window box in London. Such was its popularity that by the early nineteenth century, horticultural writer Henry Phillips wrote that while Paris might smell of freshly roasted coffee, the signature smell of London's streets was mignonette, although 'the odour which this little flower exhales is thought by some, whose olfactories are delicate, to be too powerful for the house'.[15] This was confirmed by Franco-American

Louis Simond, who wrote that during his visit to London in 1810, 'the windows are . . . universally adorned with plants quite fresh and luxuriant – the reseda particularly, which perfumes the air: this luxury is very general.'[16]

By the early nineteenth century, prolific horticultural writer John Claudius Loudon instructed his readers on how to have a constant supply of 'dwarf' and 'tree' mignonette in flower throughout the year by four sowings, one at the beginning of August, one at the end of August, one at the end of February and one at the end of May. Tree mignonette, Loudon explained, was simply the basic plant trained into a standard, which could produce plants that would last a year with correct care and pinching out. Little wonder then that many town dwellers bought their plants from nurseries. Records show that Belgian nurseries were producing 1,000 pots a week of mignonette so it is likely that English nurseries were doing the same. George Rishon of the Bedford Nursery gave a paper to the Horticultural Society on repeat sowings of the plant in 1817, since, he said, 'the demand for Mignonette in pots, at all seasons of the year, is so considerable.'[17] While some of these would have used as summer bedding in the garden and for window boxes, most would have been brought indoors as well for their delicious scent, which now sadly seems to have been bred out of the strain.

Not surprisingly, Josiah Wedgwood saw the popularity of this plant, usually grown as an annual, as yet another marketing opportunity for his chinaware. In the late eighteenth century, factory notebooks from Etruria show that there were a variety of sizes and styles of 'mignionett' pans and stands available. Early designs for this pan were labelled 'myrtle pans' but with the sudden popularity of this new, easy-to-grow plant, they were quickly relabelled. All were straight-sided bowls with matching saucers and came in the same patterns as other domestic pottery sold by Wedgwood.

Half-backed bulb pots designed to stand on the mantelpiece were also produced in a variety of sizes and matching designs, from one cup to five cups, even up to twelve cups, for holding hyacinths which were now enormously popular. Some had small holes near the cups that could be for cut flowers but are far more likely to have been for supporting sticks since hyacinths in particular are notoriously floppy and top-heavy. By the middle of the eighteenth century, Maximilien-Henri, Marquis de Saint-Simon described in his book, *Des Jacintes, de leur anatomie, reproduction, et culture* (1768), over 2,000 different varieties, most of which were doubles, that were available to keen growers.

Flower bricks, rectangular ceramic flower stem holders, were also adapted for growing small bulbs. Such were the variety and flexibility of the garden pots, flowerpots, stick flowerpots, flower bricks and pyramid flowerpots made by Wedgwood that it is difficult to know whether they were intended for growing 'roots' or bulbs, or the display of fresh flowers.

Of one design there is no doubt and those were the charming 'hedgehog' crocus pots. From the middle of the eighteenth century, the larger flowering crocus, *Crocus vernus*, was imported from Holland in vast quantities for its bright display of early spring yellow, white and purple. Snowdrops also were brought indoors for their sweet scent. Wedgwood's enthusiasm for creative designs clearly spilled over on to the factory floor, as there is an entry in one of the factory 'oven' books describing these as 'porcoipins for snowdrips'.[18] Whether growing crocuses or snowdrops or any other small bulb, these ceramic creatures must have been a talking point in any drawing room. In one month, fifty of these hedgehog crocus pots were made in black and a variety of sizes, clearly a popular design and relatively cheap at around 5*s*. 3*d*.

As with many of Wedgwood's horticultural designs, it was most probably copied, something confirmed by an article that appeared in an early issue of the *Transactions of the Horticultural Society of London*. 'Innumerable forced pots of Crocuses are seen annually exposed for sale in Covent Garden,' wrote Adrian Hardy Haworth in 1809,

> along with other vernal flowers; and a sort of pot called a Hedgehog, also often appears amongst the others. It is made in the shape of that quadruped, but full of holes, and filled with earth; and one large Crocus root is place internally, in front of every hole; the bristling leaves of which, shooting through the holes, represent grotesquely enough, but not unaptly, the spines of the animal. But I have seldom observed these crocine hedgehogs produce many flowers. This, however, may arise from their not receiving a sufficient supply of water; and if so, admits of the most easy remedy, by occasional immersion of the whole Hedgehog in a vessel of water.[19]

Wedgwood's hedgehogs came with shaped saucers to sit in, which might have made the watering simpler. There is little doubt that the creativity of Wedgwood and Bentley encouraged the popularity of growing bulbs indoors in attractive containers, which was at its peak during the end of the eighteenth and beginning of the nineteenth centuries.

In addition to Wedgwood's more elaborate designs for bulbs, he and other manufacturers such as Leeds were producing English versions of the French *cache-pot*, meaning literally 'hide-a-pot'. Particularly popular at the Sèvres factory, these were designed to disguise a basic terracotta flowerpot that could be easily changed as a flowering plant such as highly popular new introduction, the pelargonium, went over. By the 1780s, over fifty varieties of pelargoniums had arrived in Europe from the Cape of Good Hope area where they were endemic and were one of the increasing numbers of varieties of tender plants that were becoming popular for growing indoors.

Surprisingly, it is hard to find paintings of eighteenth-century interiors with these plants displayed. This was, after all, the great period for the 'conversation' piece, the family portrait which showed off stylish fashions, precious tea services and looking glasses, yet rarely does one see Wedgwood's mignonette pans let alone pyramid flowerpots or hedgehog crocus pots. It could be that that many of the eighteenth-century conversation piece portraits were exactly that – portraits of the sitter, not an accurate depiction of their living space.

It is equally difficult to find many examples of window boxes in illustrations of eighteenth-century homes and yet we also know they were there from contemporary writings. In the diary of a weekend's activities in London in the mid-eighteenth century dedicated to William Hogarth, the anonymous author of the marvellously entitled *Low-Life: or One Half of the World, Knows not how the Other Half Lives* describes the activities of the 'people about the City and Suburbs' very early one Sunday morning 'as have a Board before their Chamber-Windows, crowded with a Number of Flower-Pots, filled with Angelica, Southernwood, Pinks, Roses, &c., getting Water, and giving them a Morning's Refreshment'.[20] Modest displays these may have been, they give little hint of the explosion of interest in plants around the home that was about to happen.

CHAPTER 6

TOWN AND VILLA

Of the thousands of plant introductions in the eighteenth century, many of these were tender plants needing special housing particularly during the winter. These included the Jade plant (*Crassula arborescens*), which arrived from South Africa in 1739, *Cordyline fruticosa* from China in 1771, the first of the enormously popular cordyline family to be displayed in conservatories, and the umbrella plant (*Cyperus alternifolius*), which was introduced from Madagascar in 1781.

These tender exotics required special care and somewhere warm to display them. Coal was the preferred fuel in most homes but rooms were only heated intermittently and would not have provided a steady enough supply of warmth. While the wealthy enthusiast might have specially built 'stove' houses, this was not an option for most, but with improved building techniques it was becoming possible to have a dual-purpose structure that did more than just shelter plants.

In 1704 Queen Anne set a fashion by using her conservatory or 'greenhouse' at Kensington Palace for summer supper parties. The building was called a 'green' house because it was used for storing evergreen orange trees during the winter. Having this much space devoted to a few trees was still the prerogative of the very rich.

At first, orangeries and conservatories were rarely attached to the main house but there were beginning to be exceptions. In the 1760s, William Belchier, a banker with a home in Epsom, built one of the first glass buildings that opened out from his 'elegant drawing-room'. Belchier had covered his grove of orange and lemon trees, which were growing in the ground, with a glass 'case' allowing him to walk through his orange grove in the winter straight from his living quarters.[1] We know nothing more about this building but it must have been one of the first in the country to have a glass roof. Since glass was taxed by size, small panes made from cheaper thick glass were often used. Early conservatory glass had a faint green tint to it, giving the plants some protection from the sun's rays.

Humphry Repton (1752–1818), who took over from 'Capability' Brown as the country's leading landscape designer, discouraged his clients from having conservatories built directly attached to their homes. 'The smell and damp from a large body of earth in the beds, or pots,' he wrote, 'is often more powerful than the fragrance of the plants; therefore the conservatory should always be separated from the house, by a lobby, or small anti-room.'[2] This led to Repton being asked to design what became something of a speciality of his, the 'flower passage', a glazed tunnel linking the two, which acted as a half-way house and prevented any smells reaching the main home.

But such was the popularity of exotic plants that keen gardeners, even in cities, were anxious to have extra space in which to grow them. As prodigious horticultural writer Richard Bradley exclaimed:

> Can there be anything more agreable in the Winter, than to have a View from a Parlour or Study thorow Ranges of Orange-Trees, and curious Plants of foreign Countries, blossoming and bearing Fruit, when our Gardens without Doors are, as it were, in a State of Death?[3]

By 1816, Repton showed in verse in his *Fragments on the Theory of Landscape Gardening* that the minimalist Georgian-style drawing room was *passé*.

> No more the cedar parlour's formal gloom
> With dullness chills, 'tis now the living room,
> Where guests to whim, to task or fancy true
> Scatter'd in groups, their different plans pursue.
> Here politicians eagerly relate
> The last day's news, or the last night's debate.
> Here books of poetry and books of prints
> Furnish aspiring artists with new hints . . .
> Here, midst exotic plants, the curious maid
> Of Greek and Latin seems no more afraid.[4]

Jane Austen confirmed this in her last novel *Persuasion* (1818), writing how the 'old fashioned square parlour' was given 'the proper air of confusion by the grand piano forte and harp, flower-stands and little tables placed in every direction'.

Few went to the lengths or rather heights of George Farrant, who lived in the centre of Mayfair. We know little about Mr Farrant except that he had the wherewithal to engage one of London's busiest designers, George Tod in 1807. Tod built him a 'green-house' raised to a level with his first floor drawing room and supported by pillars above the yard below. 'There are fancy stages placed within,' described Tod, 'and the whole has a novel and pleasant appearance from the drawing-room, particularly in the evening when lighted with lamps.'[5] Other clients soon followed suit: Richard Dickinson had a greenhouse built through which one had to walk to reach his house in Golders Green. John Jackson, living in Hammersmith, had two conservatories built which adjoined the drawing room through folding glazed doors.

Although Tod was building for royalty and aristocracy – he had built a forcing house at the royal retreat at Frogmore and his client list includes dukes and viscounts – the fact that he was also commissioned by 'gentlemen' shows that glazed buildings for the growing of plants were no longer the exclusive prerogative of the wealthy. The craze for elaborate and sophisticated garden rooms was gathering momentum among the well-to-do middle classes, as exemplified by the alterations done by Tod to the existing conservatory belonging to a Mr Gosling, which adjoined the drawing room of his villa in Roehampton. Having changed the slate roof for a glass one which was less 'injurious to the growth of plants', Tod installed a screen of trellis work in alternate roof panels and on the back wall 'for the purpose of training creeping or running plants'. There were an aviary and a fountain in the middle of Mr Gosling's conservatory, with an arbour and seat immediately behind, against the back wall. Clearly there was little or nothing else like this to be found in Roehampton or nearby, since Tod described this piece of work as 'finished in a manner superior to most buildings of this description'.[6]

Sadly, we do not know what plants Mr Gosling kept in his conservatory but we can take an educated guess, since by the turn of the century many nurserymen were publishing priced lists of plants suitable for growing under glass. Several of the major London nurseries sold tender plants and were always trying to find new varieties. James Lee, who had a nursery on the site of an old vineyard in Hammersmith, is reported to have introduced around 135 new plants into England during his lifetime, including *Fuchsia coccinea*.

Fuchsias had been discovered in 1703 by the Jesuit missionary and botanist Father Carole Plumier. He later published a work describing the plants he had found in San Domingo, called *Nova Plantarum*

Americanarum Genera. In it he described what he thought of as his greatest find, which he called *Fuchsia triphylla flore coccinea.* He named the plant, as he did all his discoveries, after an influential botanist, in this case, Leonhart Fuchs, a sixteenth-century professor of medicine in Tübingen. Little more was seen or heard of the new discovery until 1788 when a Captain Firth managed to bring back *F. coccinea* from Brazil and donated it to Kew Gardens.

The commercial introduction of the same plant and in the same year is a better-known story. The nurseryman James Lee was told that a beautiful plant had been seen in a window box in Wapping, 'the flowers [hanging] in rows like tassels from the pendant branches, their colour the richest crimson, in the centre a fold of deep purple'.[7] Lee rushed to the place and persuaded the owner, the widow of a sailor – perhaps from Captain Firth's own ship – to part with the plant in return not just for money but also with the promise of fresh plants from the cuttings he intended to take. It must have been a vigorous plant because it was reported that he soon had 300 plants ready to sell. One by one, they were produced in his showroom and quickly sold for a guinea apiece to be displayed in the drawing rooms and boudoirs of his delighted clientele. Lee kept his word and replaced the widow's plant.

In contrast, auriculas were no longer so widely grown. Since no heat or other elaborate protection was needed, growers, especially in the northern working-class areas of Lancashire, had increasingly taken them up. This dented their popularity elsewhere. In 1822, John Loudon (1783–1842) wrote, '[The auricula] is like the Tulip, Pink, etc., a poor man's flower, and a fine blow is rarely seen in the gardens of the nobility and gentry.'[8] Nevertheless, in 1826, fifty auricula shows were held across the country. Throughout the nineteenth century, so many new varieties appeared that one feels they were running out of names, Clough's Do-little and Taylor's Ploughboy just two rather obscure examples.

Books appeared advising owners of conservatories and hothouses on plant care. Loudon, who took over Philip Miller's mantle in terms of horticultural writing and authority, was not optimistic. These were early days in terms of technology and Loudon felt that town gardeners, in London particularly, had more than their fair share of problems to deal with. This was especially so if they attempted to have greenhouses attached to their homes. In his manual *Green-house Companion* (1824), he positively discouraged amateurs from attempting such a thing.

No green-houseplant will ever thrive in a town where fossil coal is generally consumed. All that can be said with advantage on town green-houses might be comprised in a very few words: viz. that the only way to have them look well is to agree with a nurseryman to keep up a supply of verdant flowering plants for such a part of the year as the family is in town. We are confident there is no other mode that will be attended with success, till the nature of plants or the nature of a coal fire is considerably altered.[9]

Grim advice indeed for men such as Messrs Gosling and Jackson. But George Tod's new glass buildings hinted at the revolution that was to come in growing and displaying plants in and around the home. Those without the resources to cosset their plants in new-fangled hothouses and conservatories still had to make do with displaying their treasures inside their homes. Many would have taken Loudon's advice and restricted their choice of plants in the home to the annuals he recommended such as the ever-faithful mignonette, wallflowers, sweet peas and bulbs 'as these when they have done flowering are of no use to any one'.

For glassed-in areas, Loudon suggested growing free-flowering hardy plants such as 'Geraniums, Myrtles, Coluteas, Pittosporums, Corraeas, Acacias, and the like; and to indulge only in the hardier heaths and camellias, with but a few orange trees'. He sensibly advised that plant pot saucers should be half filled with gravel to avoid letting the plants stand in water for any length of time. If this could not be done, he advised using a large sponge to soak up any remaining water an hour after watering. Any indoor gardener will appreciate the difficulties of leaving such chores to someone else, he added, clearly indicating who would have been doing these more repetitive tasks: 'few servants can be trusted to attend to this.'[10]

With the close links between interior design themes and domestic accessories now at its peak, it was hardly surprising that furniture manufacturers also picked up on the growing popularity of displaying exotic plants indoors. Wooden staging designed for inside use became available to avid indoor gardeners, and in 1810 horticultural writer Walter Nicol gave sensible advice on how best to use these.

Plants placed on small stages, fitted to the windows, should . . . be carefully arranged . . . placing the lowest next the light, that the whole may be as much exposed to it as possible. These stages should be place on castors, in order that they may easily be moved from, or towards the light at pleasure . . . But there is another reason for having these stages on castors or pivots, that of turning them round to view the flowers at pleasure, and with ease. Also by having them placed so, they could be moved from one room to another with facility; either to take advantage of sunshine in the short days of winter, according as the rooms may be situated with respect to aspect; or from the morning parlour to the drawing-room, and the contrary. All this may be done without in the least disturbing the plants, and at an expence not worth mentioning.[11]

The expense not worth mentioning was most likely the energy of the already overworked housemaids who would have been dragooned into pushing laden staging from one room to another in search of either sunlight or an audience, all the time terrified in case one of the precious plants fell off and crashed to the floor.

Nicol, an experienced gardener from Scotland, who was known by the oddly modern-sounding description of a 'horticultural designer and author', was not finished in his advice for 'town and villa' gardeners. He continued to plead on behalf of the poor plants banished to a dark corner and rightly pointed out that the plants themselves would make it obvious they were unhappy if they were not moved into the light occasionally.

Plants placed in the lobby or hall, not perhaps near to a window, but on tables, or chairs, merely to furnish them out, and take off from their dull appearances, should never be let stand long so at a time; but should be changed to a better situation occasionally, in order to recruit health, and recover lost verdure. If we but half observe what nature points out, the plants themselves will tell what should be done. They will stretch their feeble shots towards the light, as much as to say, 'Let me see the face of the sun, the fountain of my life!'[12]

Loudon also insisted that plants brought indoors had to be kept near the light as much as possible, never overwatered but kept free from dust and dirt by regular syringing or sponging, and kept warmer than in the greenhouse. The surface of the pot was to be covered with fine fresh moss or coarse sand to lessen evaporation and all decaying parts removed. 'The management of plants in chambers', he continued, 'can only be understood to apply to the short time in which they are kept there.'

The only true way to have a fine display on the chamber-stage, is, never to bring the plants there till they are just coming into flower, and to remove them when the flowers first show indications of decay, unless the plant appears to be growing sickly before, which with heaths, geraniums, and camellias, is very often the case.[13]

If one was not completely put off by this labour-intensive care that needed to be lavished on the poor plants not expected to survive for long, then decisions had to be made as to where to buy them. Nurseries were publishing priced lists of plants suitable for growing under glass, though these were intended for the greenhouse rather than the home. Loudon suggested Covent Garden as a source. Peddlers also travelled the streets, selling plants from door to door. Some town dwellers kept a house or villa in the country where part of the gardener's job was to supply plants for the city home. Loudon still insisted that the most economical way to furnish a house with plants was to contract a nurseryman.

For those without the green fingers to look after their own plants, there were two options: to hire a gardener or to hire plants. The latter was not such an outlandish and expensive idea as it first seems. Since the late seventeenth century, nurseries had rented out space in their stove houses to protect the delicate fruit trees of wealthy owners, even royalty, who were without such provisions and expertise. It was only a small step to offer plants for hire as and when needed, especially to the wide range of clients who assembled in London for 'The Season'. There was a great deal to recommend plant contracting: why go to all the work of raising plants that were only needed for a few weeks or maybe even a few hours of the year when someone else could take the risks and provide long-term protection from the London smog? Since London was increasingly burning coal rather than wood, the air was getting filthier by the year.

The earliest mention that has been found of contract gardening was an advertisement in the London *Evening Standard* in 1747. Certainly, by the end of the eighteenth century, this is a well-established business as the records of James Cochran, nurseryman and plant hirer, show. Details of Cochran's business during the Regency period list his best customers as members of the beau monde, London's society set described by Cruikshank in his Corinthian Order of stratified society most appropriately as 'Roses, Pinks and Tulips'.[14]

Loudon's description of how rooms should be decorated with plants for parties paints a spellbinding picture of London society in the early nineteenth century. Loudon suggested that the pots be painted, chalked or covered in coloured paper. If they were only going to be used for one night then saucers were not needed and the pots could be placed on paper or small carpets. Plants were to be displayed in recesses and on side tables and in front of mirrors to reflect them. And what plants! Fruit-bearing trees were suggested for dinner parties from which 'during the dessert, the fruit is gathered by the company ... sometimes a row of orange trees, or standard peach trees, or cherries or all of them, in fruit surround the table of the guests'.[15] Hosts and hostesses tried to outdo each other with magnificent displays of flowering trees and floral troughs that would shine for the night and disappear back to Cochran's nursery the next day.

This was lucrative business: for one night in June 1818, a customer, Mr Cockrell, spent £62 on 1,240 plants and £1 10s. on the men to deliver, set up and collect them. Plants were what was wanted – only 5s. was spent on flowers that night – and all the by now familiar varieties would have been supplied: verbena, myrtle, dianthus, sweet briar, erica, heartsease, stocks and, in pride of place, dozens of plants of mignonette displayed in Wedgwood pots, stands, troughs and tin-lined boxes.

It was not just the society hostess and the conservatory owner who benefited from contracting in supplies of plants. London nurseryman James Mangles suggested that this was the only way for families 'to maintain a gay display in their windows' given the poisonous atmosphere caused by the coal being burnt in most London fires: 'no skill or art – no assiduity or care – will protect [their] plants from the destructive infection of the pernicious "*blacks*" ... By a *contract*, ... the amateur is relieved of all this trouble and uncertainty, and he will always have before him a healthy and vigorous floration.'[16]

Mr Hopgood, a nurseryman in Bayswater, supplied a nearby house with plants for the balconies of the drawing room, the dining room and the bedrooms, pots in the back and front garden and the greenhouse – 'never to have less than 70 plants, capable of containing 110' – for the sum of £69 10s. a year. This, Mangles pointed out, was only 10s. less than the average wage of one gardener including his board. Contracts would be made by the year, the quarter, the month, the week, or for the summer months only. It was particularly desirable – especially to the nurseryman – to have flowers outside the bedroom balconies, Mangles suggested, 'as besides their graceful appearance from within, the sight of them on getting up in the morning is the most cheering object we can behold.' There were nurseries across London that provided such services, as well as supplying the usual bedding for window boxes such as mignonette at 6s. a dozen and geraniums at 10s. each.[17]

The lack of variety offered by Cochran and Mangles when amateur greenhouses across the country were beginning to bulge with rare exotics is hardly a surprise. Cochran and other nurserymen were in the business of supplying stylish, reliable plants that were easy to grow. With a high mortality rate, they could not afford to lavish care on rarities – that was left to the enthusiast. And for the enthusiast, these were exciting times.

CHAPTER 7

'THE LARGEST HOT-HOUSE
IN THE WORLD'

The nineteenth century was a boom time for indoor gardening. Advances in travel and technology changed the way people lived and worked and that affected everyone from gardeners and nurserymen to housewives. In Britain, the railways linked cities and towns across the country and allowed goods to be transported at speeds never dreamt of before. In the late 1820s, an excited market garden editorial exclaimed that 'if a railroad were laid down on one side of the common road, the travelling between all the grand points, as London, Edinburgh, Glasgow, . . . might be performed at a rate of 24 miles an hour. The cheapness of this mode of travelling is not less remarkable than its rapidity.'[1] Within a few years, this had become a reality, and it was possible to transport plants from nurseries to city markets such as Covent Garden with relative ease, and then forward them from these markets to estates and homes across the country.

These were also exciting times across the world. The end of the Seven Years' War in 1763 had given Britain dominance on the seas and allowed trading posts to open up in India, the Far East, the West Indies and Canada. The fabled voyage of Captain Cook's *Endeavour* and Sir Joseph Banks's many discoveries in Australia and New Zealand paved the way for a century of staggering horticultural exploration. Banks's expeditions gave enterprising botanists the impetus to travel further than ever before in what was becoming the golden age of plant hunting. This was spurred on by financial backing from entrepreneurial nurserymen back home in England. Professional encouragement also came from the still young horticultural organizations of Kew Botanical Gardens, which Banks ran unofficially for around forty years, and the Horticultural Society. Both of these achieved 'royal' status in the early nineteenth century.

Yet one of the great problems facing all these plant hunters was the task of transporting sample plants back to Britain. For centuries, botanists had usually had to make do with growing new discoveries from seed, such as those sent over in 'Bartram's boxes', since cuttings invariably died on the long sea journeys home. The disadvantage to this was that seeds are only produced at certain times of the year and could not be guaranteed to be viable. Enterprising explorers attempted to pot up plants that were then strung up in ships' cabins for the journey home. But sea captains, reluctant to give up either valuable space or fresh water, were rarely sympathetic to transporting dozens of fragile plants this way and few made it back to Britain. Given all these difficulties it is astounding that thousands of new species had arrived in Britain in the eighteenth century.

All that was to change due mainly to two men's inventiveness. There are few horticultural legends that are as well known as that of the discovery of the benefits of glass plant-cases, best known as the Wardian case. The truth is that the man who first experimented with sealed cases was Scottish botanist and professor of law at Glasgow University Alexander Maconochie. He had experimented with growing exotic ferns and club mosses that he had obtained from the Glasgow Botanic Garden in 1825. For fourteen years, he grew them in an old goldfish tank and, although his experiments were known among his circle of friends, sadly by the time he published his findings, someone else had beaten him to it. The case built by Londoner Dr Ward was already public knowledge. Graciously Maconochie passed the honours to the doctor.

Dr Nathaniel Bagshaw Ward (1791–1868) was the son of a GP in London's Whitechapel. Following in his father's footsteps as a doctor, Ward attended lectures at the Chelsea Physic Garden. He was inspired by stories of plant-hunting expeditions into the countryside to become an amateur botanist in his spare time, rising at dawn to botanize before seeing his patients. Ward struggled to garden at his home in Wellclose Square in the docklands area of the East End because of the airborne pollution. In 1830, attempting to protect a chrysalis in a bottle, he noticed two seedlings had sprouted in the surrounding soil and appeared to be thriving. And thrive they did – for nineteen years in the same bottle on Ward's windowsill.

So motivated was Ward by this discovery that he started experimenting with different designs of miniature greenhouses, always aiming for 'a moist atmosphere free from soot or other extraneous particles; light, heat, moisture and periods of rest and change of air'.[2] By 1833 he had managed to grow not only thirty different ferns under glass but also the epiphyte *Asplenium nidus*, the bird's-nest fern.

The greatest test, however, was to be using one of his greenhouses on a long-distance journey. In June 1833, Ward joined forces with his friend and nurseryman, George Loddiges, to send two cases filled with ferns and grasses on board a ship bound for Sydney, Australia. In November 1834, they finally heard that the plants arrived in perfect health – a lesson to remind us how long these journeys took and what patience was required. In February 1835, the little cases were refilled with a variety of plants including the coral fern (*Gleichenia microphylla*) and Australian black wattle (*Callicoma serratifolia*).

Gleichenia was discovered in 1810 in China but had never survived the journey to Britain. The return journey passed through snow in Rio de Janeiro and temperatures of over 38°C at the equator, and took eight months. One can imagine the state of excitement of the two men as they boarded the ship to inspect the much-travelled glass cases and their precious contents. 'I will not readily forget the delight expressed by Mr George Loddiges, who accompanied me on board,' wrote Dr Ward, 'at the beautiful appearance of *Gleichenia microphylla*, a plant now seen for the first time alive in this country.'[3]

The garden writer John Loudon visited Dr Ward's home in Whitechapel and saw for himself how revolutionary the doctor's designs were. Immediately he published a report of Ward's experiments in his best-selling horticultural journal, the *Gardener's Magazine*.

> The success attending to Mr Ward's experiments opens up extensive views as to other applications in transporting plants from one place to another; in preserving plants in rooms, or in towns; and in forming miniature gardens or conservatories . . . as substitutes for bad views, or for no views at all.[4]

He then persuaded Dr Ward, by nature a modest man, to write about his experiments in the next issue of his magazine.

Ward's ideas were quickly taken up by the horticultural world, especially those trying to bring back plants from far away. This detailed explanation of how a consignment of tender green houseplants was packed for delivery from Calcutta to England was written by Captain R. Gillies of the ship *Hibernia* and published in 1839.

> Each plant was in a box, six inches square by one foot in depth, filled to the top with a kind of clay, and no doubt well saturated with water, previously to being put into the large outer box, which contained eight of these small ones. The large box was

constructed in the usual way, that is, a glazed roof about two feet high, the glass strong enough to resist the fall of a small rope, or other large body. It was hermetically sealed with the common lime cement of the country and was never opened during a voyage of five months. When we arrived in England, the plants were all in beautiful health, and had grown to the full height of the case, the leaves pressing against the glass.[5]

The captain observed that even in dry weather there was always moisture within the glass that he assumed was absorbed by the plants. Nevertheless, he was puzzled and found it difficult to account for the perfect health of the plants, but suggested that enough oxygen passed through the 'pores of the wood' for them not just to survive but thrive. 'No water was given to them during the voyage,' he asserted, '[yet] they were landed in excellent order.'[6]

Not surprisingly, Ward was also encouraged to give talks but it was not until 1842 that a fully detailed account was published entitled *On the Growth of Plants in Closely Glazed Cases*. 'Closely' was a key word since Captain Gillies was correct and Ward's cases were never designed to be completely airtight. The process by which plants could survive in such conditions was still not completely understood, even by Dr Ward, but it is no exaggeration to say that its discovery changed the face of horticulture worldwide. It allowed crops such as tea to be established in India from China, rubber plants from South America to be transported to Malaya, and banana trees from China to Fiji. From the late 1830s, the Royal Botanical Gardens at Kew, which was at that time run by Ward's friend William Jackson Hooker (whose son Joseph Dalton Hooker was among the first plant collectors to use this invention on his plant-hunting expeditions), used Ward's techniques for propagation for over a hundred years. Even as new technologies have improved things, anyone who has ever popped a cutting into a plastic bag owes a debt to Ward – and Maconochie – for their curiosity.

Ward's friend George Loddiges, who had arranged that first visit to Australia to test out the plant-case's suitability for long-distance travel, was the son of Joachim Conrad Loddiges. He ran a nursery that horticultural historian John Harvey has called 'outstandingly important for its introductions of hothouse exotics' in the late eighteenth century.[7] Joachim Conrad Loddiges had taken over the original small nursery from his friend Joseph Busch when the latter became gardener to

Catherine the Great in Russia. Under Loddiges's care, the nursery began specializing in finding, raising, selling and even exporting rare exotic plants. As the Hackney Botanic Nursery, it became the focal point for the introduction and study of rare plants. In the early nineteenth century, 200 examples provided by the nursery were illustrated as fine coloured plates in the *Botanical Magazine*, started by renowned horticulturalist William Curtis.

George, Joachim Conrad's youngest son, who was to become so involved with Dr Ward and his glass cases just a few years later, was fully involved with the nursery as it entered its golden period between 1820 and 1840. George Loddiges went on to build one of the earliest steam-heated stove houses in the country. The Royal Horticultural Society awarded him a medal in 1817 for his ingenious rain sprinkler system that used perforated pipes attached to the hothouse eaves. It was used particularly to house and cosset the tender Mauritius fan palm (*Latania lontaroides*), which the nursery had acquired in 1814.

By 1821, plans were afoot to build a larger house 'for the growth of palms'. Known as the Grand Palm House, it allowed palms, epiphytic orchids and other exotics to be grown as never before, as this description from 1833 shows:

In the palm house everything is in its usual luxuriance; the ferns are in most vigorous growth and the epiphytes flowering beautifully. *Oncidium divaricatum* and *flexuosum* and *Calthe veratrifolia* are extremely conspicuous. There is a beautiful new Lycopidium (*L. circinatum*), the thick-set branches of which can only compare to fine chenille work in embroidery. A shower of rain was let off to show the effect to a stranger who accompanied us. We mention this to remind our readers of what has been done in this way and what may be done again in lofty conservatories.[8]

Few owners of 'lofty' or not so lofty conservatories would have been able to emulate the wonders of Loddiges's Hackney Botanic Nursery. The catalogue value of the plants at the nursery was estimated at £200,000 in 1829 and the collection was by no means complete at that stage. Joseph Paxton (1803–65), the famed gardener and architect, was employed to design yet another new palm house. His use of wood in a curved roof in this palm house predated the later hothouse he built at Chatsworth for the display of the first *Victoria Regia* (now *amazonica*) lily in 1849, and the Crystal Palace, built in 1851 to house the Great Exhibition.

Loddiges specialized in exotic plants for the greenhouse and conservatory, including camellias still thought to be tender. So successfully did they grow in the enormous Hackney greenhouse that the *Gardener's Magazine* of 1833 reported that it had become 'a complete wood of that shrub, so much so that blackbirds have repeatedly built their nests and reared their young in it'.[9] It is no wonder that Loudon called it 'the largest hot-house in the world'.

A visit to the Loddiges's tropical hothouses in Hackney, still a relatively green and undeveloped area of east London, became a 'must-do' visit for local middle-class families. William Allen, a Quaker chemist living in nearby Stoke Newington, took his cousin Emily G. Birkbeck and a friend, Anna Hanbury, there on 30 March 1822, and described the sights.

> We all went to Loddiges Nursery, to see the camellias which are now in full bloom and very beautiful! There is quite a forest of them: his hot-houses are, perhaps the most capacious in the world: one of them is 40 feet high: in this there is a banana tree which nearly reaches the top.[10]

Camellias had originally come from China and Japan and were named posthumously by Linnaeus after George Joseph Kamel, a Moravian missionary. He had sent plant specimens back from his travels in the Pacific, though apparently never camellias. The first camellias in Britain were grown by Lord Petrie, a passionate gardener who had a flowering *Camellia japonica* among his collection of exotics in the mid-eighteenth century at his home at Thornden Hall in Essex.

By the early nineteenth century, several variations of *C. japonica* were available and enormously popular, but as it was still thought that they were tender, many perished in the overheated conditions of the early 'stove' houses. In 1842, the *Ladies' Magazine of Gardening*, written by Jane Loudon, the young wife of J. C. Loudon, recommended growing them in pots, claiming they were 'very nearly hardy' thought they will not 'bear the open air far north of London'.[11]

By then, the enormous popularity of camellias was at its peak. 'The number of Camellias raised every year both in England and on the Continent almost exceeds belief; and in America they are so highly prized as ornaments for the hair, &c., that a dollar is the common price for a single flower,' reported the *Ladies' Magazine of Gardening*.[12] So for those living north of Watford who wanted to be part of the camellia mania of the early nineteenth century, there was little choice. While the Duke of Devonshire was able to commission Joseph Paxton to build him camellia houses at both Chatsworth and at Chiswick House, others were not so fortunate. But where there is a will, there is a way, and one year before, in 1841, a Mrs Glover who lived in Pearsall Cottage near Wolverhampton told readers of the *Ladies' Magazine* that she had camellias 'now beautifully in flower, that have been kept in my living-room for several years'.[13]

Orchids also caught the horticultural public's imagination and were magnificently grown by Loddiges. *Bletia purpurea*, one of the first exotic, as opposed to native, orchids to arrive in Britain, had been sent to Peter Collinson from the Bahamas in 1731. In 1798, the botanic garden at Kew had fifteen species and within fifteen years this has grown to eighty-four.

But this was nothing compared to what was to come. In 1818, a plant hunter called William Swainson packed up some exotics to send back from an exploration in Brazil using, in these pre-Wardian days, some rather uninteresting-looking plant material as protection. When they arrived back in England, they were unpacked by William Cattley, who, rather than discarding the unknown packing materials, thought he would try and grow them on – with enormous success.

The resulting flowers were so astoundingly beautiful that they triggered the orchid fever that gripped nineteenth-century collectors and a few still today. The plant was named *Cattleya labiata* after Cattley by John Lindley, who was by then the assistant secretary of the Horticultural Society and professor of botany at University College, London, and has been called the father of modern orchidology.

Not surprisingly, the Hackney Botanic Nursery was the first to cultivate orchids on a commercial basis and a later discovery was named after George Loddiges: *Cattleya loddigesii*. It remains one of the most popular orchids to this day, which is appropriate considering how much the Loddiges family, and George in particular, contributed to the cultivation of orchids during the mid-nineteenth century. From a list of eighty-four species in 1825, they were able to offer over 1,600 species by 1839.

Unfortunately, many varieties of orchids were lost as plant hunters plundered the rain forests of South America. Of those that were bought from the nursery to be grown as houseplants, few survived since few amateur gardeners had the knowledge to promote flowering and, discouraged, many just threw their plants away. Sir Joseph Banks called the period from 1800 to 1820 'the grave of tropical orchids'.[14] However, in spite of this, there are still about 25,000 different species of orchids and over 100,000 hybrids in cultivation.

With so many more exotic plants now arriving in Britain needing protection during the colder months, storage and display became major issues. For the wealthy aristocrat, price was not a problem. The tax on glass throughout the eighteenth century and up until 1845 kept prices high. A crate of 'crown' glass, preferred by gardeners to 'broad' glass because of its flatness, cost £12 before 1845 but dropped to £2 8s. after the repeal of the tax. Both types of glass had a greenish tinge which gave plants some protection from direct sun but they could only be made in relatively small sizes.

Sheet glass which was made from 1831 on the other hand, together with the invention of a curvilinear wrought iron glazing bar by J. C. Loudon, was set to revolutionize the construction of glasshouses and bring them within the reach of the demanding middle classes. When the price of sheet glass fell from a pre-repeal price of 1s. 2d. a foot to 2d. a foot, there was no excuse for every aspiring homeowner not to have his own conservatory attached to his suburban villa with a greenhouse at the bottom of the garden.

Plants for the house were now readily available not just from nurseries such as Loddiges's Hackney Botanic but also from flower markets such as Covent Garden, and street sellers. Plants that could cope with the oppressively dark and smoky atmosphere of Victorian homes were particularly popular, such as the ubiquitous Kentia palm, *Howea forsteriana*. Peddlers called 'botany bens' knocked on servants' doors offering cheap geraniums for sale. For the rest of century, no self-respecting windowsill or conservatory was without its scented-leaved or brightly coloured pelargoniums.

A wide variety of large-flowering pelargoniums were bred through systematic hybridizing and crossing, particularly of what are popularly known as 'Zonals', which had originally been introduced by the Duchess of Beaufort in 1704. At the start of the nineteenth century, there were three major London nurseries able to supply a variety of pelargonium plants: James Colvill in Chelsea's King's Road, Andrew Henderson at Pine Apple Place in Edgware Road and Lee and Kennedy at the Vineyard Nursery in Hammersmith. Colvill's nursery in particular had a large collection, which enabled Robert Sweet, who worked for Colvill, to compile five volumes of Geraniaceae between 1820 and 1830. Sweet began this work using *P. ciconium zonale*, introduced in 1710, and *P. ciconium inquinans* (1714).

From 1840 to 1855 there was, according to the popular garden writer Shirley Hibberd (1825–90), a mania for raising scarlet pelargoniums, such as 'Frogmore Scarlet', 'Huntsman' and 'Cooper's Scarlet'. The most famous was 'General Tom Thumb'. Thrown in the dustbin as a seedling, it was rescued by one Mr Willson, gardener to W. Pigett, Esq. of Newmarket and, according to Hibberd, soon 'vanquished' its competitors. These scarlet pelargoniums became so widely propagated and widely available that soon even the poorest of homes sported a 'General' on its windowsill. By the end of the Industrial Revolution, whether it was the dusty aspidistra in the dark corner of a suburban drawing room or the bright red pelargonium on a cottage windowsill, plants had become an integral part of all British domestic interiors.

CHAPTER 8

FLORA DOMESTICA

In 1823 an anonymous book was published in London entitled *Flora Domestica, or the Portable Flower-Garden with directions for the treatment of Plants in Pots*. Two more editions appeared over the next eight years, both with additions to this useful guide to 200 flowers that could be grown in pots rather than in the ground. We know now that the book was written by Elizabeth Kent, whose sister was married to Leigh Hunt, the essayist and writer. Kent lived close by the Hunt family whose circle included Keats and Shelley, near Hampstead Heath, an area gradually being drawn into the fringes of outer London.

Elizabeth Kent's book was aimed at town dwellers like herself who had scant knowledge of plant care. With a charming honesty, she admitted to having seen her plants die 'one after the other, rather from attention ill-directed than from the want of it'. She knew she was not alone: 'Even Myrtles and Geraniums, commonly as they are seen in flower-stands, balconies, &c., often meet with an untimely death from the ignorance of their nurses.'[1] She sensed that in spite of the keen interest in gardening across Britain, that for every enthusiastic green-fingered gardener, there were a hundred more who were not and needed guidance. She also had the foresight to tap into the 'new' city gardener, echoing Thomas Fairchild's advice from a hundred years' before.

> Many a plant have I destroyed [until] I resolved to obtain and communicate such information as should be requisite for the rearing and preserving a *portable garden* in pots . . . Some even of the most scientific botanists prefer a domestic garden of this kind. For example, Richard Anthony Salisbury, Esq. the universally acknowledged head of our English botanists, no longer cultivates his former gardens at Chapel Allerton, Yorkshire, or at Mill Hill, Middlesex, but confines his attention to a choice collection of the most curious plants in pots, arranged in the yard of his house in Queen Street, Edgeware Road.[2]

The idea that any keen botanist should want to downsize from two large gardens to a courtyard garden may seem strange, but Kent was spot on in tapping into the new desire among town dwellers and middle-class homeowners in particular to be part of the fashion for floral displays. An etching by George Cruikshank from the *Comic Almanack* in the late 1830s called 'May – All A-Growing!' shows young families exchanging old clothes for potted plants from passing peddlers.

Any passionate 'plant-o-holic' would sympathize with the writer of this letter to the *Ladies' Magazine of Gardening* in 1842, based near Connaught Square near London's Marble Arch.

> I have no garden, but as I have a large balcony, I have many greenhouse plants, which look very well during summer, but which give me a great deal of trouble in winter. I have been obliged to line all my windows with them, and I have flower-stands full of them in all the living rooms; but there are still many which I am quite at a loss to dispose of. As it is neither agreeable nor wholesome to sleep with plants in the room, I cannot put them in the bed-rooms; and some that I placed in a spare attic, though I have been told that the upper rooms of the house are the warmest, were frozen. We keep horses, and, consequently, I can easily obtain manure; but this is of little use, as I have no hotbed frame, and the expense of purchasing one would be more than my plants are worth.[3]

The suggested reply of a do-it-yourself frame knocked together by a carpenter and lined with manure with old carpet hung over may not have been much appreciated. But it was just the sort of practical advice given to thousands of middle-class gardeners by Jane Loudon (1803–58), as already mentioned.

Although crippled by early illness, J. C. Loudon travelled Europe developing his ideas on greenhouse building and gathering material for his magisterial *Encyclopaedia of Gardening*. This was first published in 1822 and ran to nearly 1,500 pages covering everything from botany, garden design and plant culture to a world survey of the history of gardening. Six editions appeared during Loudon's lifetime and it continued to be published up until the 1870s.

In 1826, Loudon began publishing the *Gardener's Magazine*, the first aimed at the middle-class amateur gardener, aided by his young wife. Jane had published before she met her husband but knew nothing of horticulture. Throughout the 1830s they worked as a team, travelling together, with Jane all the time learning as she went. When she published her own work, *Instructions in Gardening for Ladies* in 1840, such was the thirst for this sort of knowledge that she sold 1,350 copies on the first day of publication, an achievement any author would be delighted with. When her husband died in 1843 leaving Jane with debts due to an overambitious publishing commitment, *Arboretum*, she continued to write and publish on gardening to support herself and her young daughter.

Neither Elizabeth Kent, who never married and made her living – albeit a meagre one – as a writer, nor Jane Loudon fit the stereotype of the Victorian middle-class wife. With a new young queen on the throne, the ideal of domestic bliss with the central figure of the *pater familias* surrounded by an adoring family is hard to dislodge. The new suburban homes that were built catered for this large but nevertheless nuclear family. With improved rail and travel networks, husbands no longer had to work close to home and so were regularly out of the house from early morning to evening. Whereas in the eighteenth century, it was usually the man of the house who made the decisions about furniture buying and decorations, these were now coming into the wife's sphere of influence. While the husband would have paid for the construction of the conservatory or the greenhouse, it was the wife who would have had the time to look after this new status symbol, with the aid of servants and jobbing gardeners as well. This was clear from a piece in the *Gentleman's Magazine*.

The nurture of exotics not only belongs more particularly to the female province, on account of its being an elegant *home* amusement, but because of there being much delicate work, essential to the welfare of plants, that is more dexterously performed by the pliant fingers of women, than by the clumsy paws of men. Ladies can also more conveniently attend the regulation of the green-house sashes, which require closer attention than the ordinary concerns of gentlemen will allow them to pay.[4]

While this sounds like a canny way of passing over the tedious work to female hands, it did fit in well with the increasing popularity of botany as a respectable accomplishment for young ladies. Together with botanical drawing, the growing and care of plants in the home fitted perfectly into the increasingly restrictive lifestyle of the suburban wife.

The management of plant pots in the home was certainly seen as female work though some clearly had other ideas.

> I have always found that, with the aid of a manservant, who, although perfectly ignorant of gardening and plants, was always ready to work where I was directing, and the still more frequent assistance of a female domestic, I could get through all the labour of managing my indoor plants.[5]

This was written by the anonymous author of *Every Lady's Guide to her own greenhouse, hothouse and conservatory*, later identified as Louisa Johnson, making it strikingly clear that this was her domain. Any ignorant manservant or wayward domestic could be easily handled.

> If domestic servants are used for purposes not immediately within the terms of their engagements, it is easy to sweeten their labours at a small expense, and the luxury of being mistress in your own place is so great that it is worth all it costs.[6]

There was no shortage of domestic labour available, which was just as well. Most middle-class households supported one or two live-in staff. While families such as these would not have needed to employ a full-time gardener, jobbing gardeners, visiting once a week or even once a month, would have taken care of any heavy work.

Jane Loudon makes a clear distinction between plants grown for the house and those needing the heat of a stove house. She did not appear to have so much faith in her female readers when it came to hothouses since she advises them against venturing into such male territory 'as the most tender kinds of stove plants cannot be grown well without the aid of a regular gardener'.[7]

There was no shortage of advice for female horticulturalists. *The Housekeeper's Receipt Book or, The Repository of Domestic Knowledge*, an early Mrs Beeton-style advice manual, was full of suggestions for the care and correct watering of flowerpots in sitting rooms, suggesting perhaps not wisely that:

> when the plants are attacked by any kind of crawling insects, the evil may be prevented by keeping the saucers full of water so as to form a river round the pot, and rubbing some oil round the side. Oil is fatal to many kinds of insects, and but few of them can endure it.[8]

Whether the plants would have survived sitting in saucers of water is another matter.

Another cautionary note was added by James Mangles in *The Floral Calendar*, which rings as true as it did nearly 200 years ago.

In purchasing flowers in pots, it is important to recollect, that by far the greater number of them have been forced into a premature display for their beauties by artificial heat and shelter, which renders them full of sap and tender, from the branches and shoots not being ripened . . . Another important circumstance is, that the nurseryman's green-house always has light perpendicular, as well as on both sides so that his plants grow upright, and send out branches on all sides, forming what is termed a well balanced head.[9]

Not surprisingly, once the plants were transferred into 'the inside of a room window, or to a flower-stand in a sitting room', the poor plants objected to the lack of light from all sides and became straggly and weakened unless the plant was turned regularly – possibly another job for the already overworked domestic.

Jane Loudon's books, on the other hand, were full of extremely practical and sensible advice that is still relevant: do not overwater indoor plants but water regularly when they begin to dry out, do not let them stand in water, do not overpot but pot up regularly though not when plants are in flower, use the correct compost or 'mould' as she called it, and finally protect against insects, especially aphids and red spider mites. Sensibly and presciently, Mrs Loudon did not approve of the use of fumigating bellows. Instead she advocated washing with a sponge and regular spraying with water: 'as it has been often observed that neither the green fly nor the red spider will ever infest a plant that is frequently syringed.'[10]

What the Loudons tapped into was the thirst for knowledge by the ever-expanding middle classes who saw plants and their accompanying decorative accessories as part of the jigsaw puzzle that was social one-upmanship. To have a conservatory implied that one had enough money to employ gardening staff to tend to the plants inside. Similarly all displays of flowers and plants, whether at the windows, in pots by the doors, or in the public rooms of the home such as the parlour, showed that there was not just a certain degree of financial status but also horticultural knowledge on display.

Given Elizabeth Kent's confession of ignorance in looking after her houseplants, it is not surprising following Nathaniel Ward's discovery that plants could virtually look after themselves in one of his cases that they were quickly taken up as the ideal way to grow easy greenery indoors. There were two other reasons why the idea of growing plants in a sealed environment became so popular in the mid-nineteenth century. The first was to do with an improvement in technology within the home that was good for the human inhabitants (if treated with care) but bad for the growing of plants. Gas lighting was gradually taken up in homes across the country. Candles were increasingly expensive and oil was dirty; their portability made them dangerous as well.

In towns where large gasworks were constructed, even modest new homes could be lit with this new-fangled lighting device. By 1822, there were forty-seven gasometers in Britain and a few large country estates had their own private gas supply. However, the technology was in its early stages and the price to pay for these early adopters was that the lamps frequently smoked a great deal and the fumes given off, apart from smelling, were fairly deadly to any plants growing in the room. Wisely, Mrs Beeton recommended 'the necessity of good ventilation in rooms lighted by gas'.[11]

The second reason was that there was still confusion over the actually benefits or ill effects of having living plants growing inside the home. An anxious reader from Turnham Green wrote to the *Ladies' Magazine of Gardening* in 1841 seeking clarification. 'I have been told that it is very dangerous to keep plants in my bedroom, but that I may keep them safely in my sitting-room. Is this the case? And if it is, what is the reason?'[12] It is not surprising that she was confused.

By the second half of the eighteenth century, the idea that plants had respiratory systems was closely explored. Experiments were conducted to test of dangers of unventilated rooms, particularly in town houses. Live plants in particular were thought to give off noxious 'effluvia', that is dangerous vapours. In 1764, a story had appeared in the *Gentleman's Magazine* about a young woman in Germany who had died after sleeping with a pot of violets by her bedside. 'The too common practice of placing pots filled with vegetating flowers, in rooms commonly used to sit in, or entertain company' was clearly to be avoided, the author suggested.[13] In contrast, the work of Sir Joseph Priestley, member alongside Josiah Wedgwood of the Lunar Society and discoverer of oxygen, showed that 'no vegetable grows in vain . . . every individual plant is serviceable to mankind . . . which cleanses out atmosphere. In this the fragrant rose and the deadly nightshade co-operate.'[14]

By the 1840s it was understood that plants could transpire through photosynthesis but the full benefits of their air-cleaning qualities were still not fully understood. In answer to the anxious lady from Turnham Green, Jane Loudon replied that she was correct in thinking that it was safe to keep plants in living rooms but not in bedrooms. This was because, she explained,

> when plants are exposed to a strong light their leaves absorb a great portion of carbonic acid gas which . . . they give out as oxygen . . . in the darkness of the night their leaves give out carbonic acid gas . . . and as a superabundance of this gas produces stupor, head-aches, and a sense of suffocation in those that breathe it, plants often produce these evil effects on those who keep them in bedrooms.[15]

This was later refuted by Florence Nightingale who claimed,

> No one ever saw 'overcrowding' by plants in a room or ward . . .the carbonic acid they give off at night would not poison a fly. Nay in overcrowded rooms, they actually absorb carbonic acid, and give off oxygen.[16]

The young Victorians therefore faced a dilemma. On the one hand, the lasting effects of the scare stories about plant and flower vapours having the ability to kill in one's own bed overnight or, at the very least, be unhealthy (an old wives' tale that lasted well into the twentieth century) led many plant owners, or rather their servants, to go through elaborate plant-moving sessions each evening. Gas fumes were so noxious at this time that few plants other than palms and the soon to be ubiquitous aspidistra would survive.

However, the popularity of botany and the fashion for plant collecting meant that the desire to bring plants into the home to care for and show off had never been stronger, hence the immediate domestic popularity of glass plant-cases for the home. Ward's case, based on a miniature greenhouse design, was copied in garden and home furnishing catalogues and produced with legs, without legs, with internal trays, without – but always ornately decorated. Jane Loudon admitted that 'as far as my own opinion goes, I confess I am no friend to plants in glass cases. They have a confined unhealthy look through the dingy glass, which is repugnant to all my ideas of floral beauty.'[17] Nevertheless she was happy to list ferns and mosses that would succeed in such cases.

As plants became part of serious home decoration, a burgeoning trade grew in producing more and more elaborate pieces of furniture on which to display them. Domestic interior historian Peter Thornton has said that the *jardinière* was even more prevalent in the 1820s than the cocktail-cabinet in the 1930s. Firms such as Wedgwood and Royal Doulton regularly produced large elaborate pieces to suit the growing market. For balcony displays, Mrs Loudon recommended double pots, usually one that fitted inside another, though occasionally they were made as one piece. The layer in between could be stuffed with moss which would insulate the inner pot both from drying winds on balconies and, if kept damp, from overheating by the sun.

In 1848, Jane Loudon published a pictorial record of plants she recommended for 'ladies' to grow as ornamental greenhouse plants. Of the 185 varieties described, Mrs Loudon insisted that she only mentioned such 'plants as may be set out in the open air during the summer or at any rate, that may be placed in a ... room when in flower'.[18]

The distinction between the uses of the conservatory, the greenhouse and the stove- or hothouse was becoming increasingly clear. The conservatory was usually attached to the house, in which plants were usually planted directly into earth beds, and seen as an extra 'room' of the home. The hot-house was for the specialist grower of exotic species that usually required a great deal of time, money and care and more constant heat than would be available in the main house.

The greenhouse, however, had come within the financial reach of most middle-class families and was seen as an invaluable space in which to raise plants, which were then brought into the home when in flower. Pride might dictate that this space was kept full of interesting specimens. But essentially it was a horticultural workroom and as such a more private space not usually shown to visitors, as a hot-house might be, or used for entertaining, as conservatories were.

In 1845, Jane Loudon wrote an advice manual aimed at young women setting up home for the first time. In it she advised them to have just a few potted plants indoors until the flower garden was made.

Remember though, you must only have a few plants, as more than five or six would give the window the appearance of being a substitute for a greenhouse, a most unpleasant idea at any time, and particularly so in the country. Two rather tall and spreading geraniums, with showy trusses of flowers, a fine well-trained Sollya heterophylla, a fine Polygala oppositifolia, and two handsome well-grown Fuchsias, will be quite enough.[19]

Unusually for Jane Loudon, this time she appears to have been out of tune with her readers. Such a small number of indoor plants would have been frowned upon. Fuchsias in particular were becoming enormously popular. Sponsored plant-hunting expeditions had brought home varieties such as *F. arborescens* (1824) and *F. fulgens* (1830). After the introduction of *F. magellanica* in 1827, hybridizing began in earnest. In 1848, a French fuchsia specialist, M. Felix Porcher, published the second edition of his book *Le Fuchsia, son histoire et sa culture* and described 520 varieties. While some have since proved to be duplicates with confusion over French and English names, others – including doubles and striped varieties – followed.

Breeders such as James Lye, who was head gardener to the Earl of Radnor's sister in Wiltshire, spent their working lives developing more and more splendid hybrids. Many are still grown though rarely to the standards of the late nineteenth century when plants trained into pyramids could reach ten feet (3 m) high smothered in flowers from top to bottom. And they were not just for the conservatory: Elizabeth Kent, writing in *Flora Domestica* in 1823, had highly recommended this 'elegant plant for the drawing-room or study'.[20]

By the mid-nineteenth century, British homes were in the grip of a horticultural hysteria. Whether it was orchid fever, camellia crazes or fuchsia fantasias, middle-class families now were seized by a green-fingered fervour in their attempts to out-plant their next-door neighbour.

CHAPTER 9

RUS IN URBE

As the cities of Britain grew, fingers of suburban streets spread out from overcrowded centres. It is estimated that six million new homes were built during Queen Victoria's reign. Whereas at the start of the nineteenth century, only 20 per cent of the population lived in cities, by the second half of the century, 54 per cent did. Many of the millions of homes now had regular water supplies and improved sewage controls. The Public Health Act of 1848 recommended that all homes should have fixed sanitary facilities and by 1865 London's new sewage system designed by Sir Joseph Bazalgette was opened. The gentle doctor, Nathaniel Ward, and dynamic George Loddiges had both lobbied for the abolition of the glass tax, which had finally been repealed in 1845.

This urban development caused casualties: Loddiges's famous Hackney nursery closed in 1854. George Loddiges had died in 1846, his older brother shortly after. George's son Conrad, who inherited the business, was a trained horticulturalist but was not able to renegotiate the leases on the nursery's land, which was swallowed up in development for homes. But the people who moved into these homes were captivated by the availability of plants now open to them.

There was no shortage of nurseries to supply these keen indoor gardeners. In 1853, James Veitch the Elder bought the Exotic Nursery in King's Road, Chelsea. The Veitch Nursery was to become the most famous commercial starting point for plant hunting until the First World War and supplied countless new varieties of plants, in particular orchids, to an ever-enthusiastic horticultural public.

Lesser nurserymen operated across London and at Covent Garden, selling their plants out in the open on the streets. Richard Weatherall from Finchley specialized in palms, pot roses and solanums, George Beckwith in pelargoniums, fuchsias and bouvardias, and another two firms in Finchley, Shoults and Kay, also specialized in pelargoniums.

Unfortunately, air pollution from the coal dust, burnt in millions of fire grates and factory chimneys, was getting worse. This problem was not just restricted to the winter months, as this passage from Mrs Haweis's *The Art of Decoration* published in 1881 shows:

> Many people object to windows being much open during the summer on account of the invasion of blacks. Many years ago I tried nailing up a guard of thin strong muslin, coloured red or green, which is certainly rather useful in defeating the largest sootflakes. It should be often changed otherwise the soot with which it is charged detaches itself by its own weight.[1]

Heavy curtaining therefore was not just a design preference but also offered some protection from the filth floating about in the air. Regrettably it also cut out the amount of light that came into the rooms. This was in some way compensated for by the arrival of the incandescent gas mantle and, in a few homes, incandescent electric light bulbs – a bonus for the families if not for the plants.

In response to the pains and pleasures of trying to grow plants in the home, a continual stream of advice books appeared. This was helped by the easing of restrictive paper taxes and improved printing technology. It was a boom time for publishing. In the second half of the nineteenth century you could take any combination of words such as stove-house, greenhouse, conservatory, exotic, foliage, fern and you would find dozens of books to answer your needs. Magazines flourished as well; gardening, as a hobby, had never been more popular.

By 1885 there were eight weekly gardening magazines and several monthlies. Some of these were aimed at professionals but most were for the keen amateur and started the trend of horticultural publishing, which is still going strong. The suburban garden was highly labour intensive with elaborate bedding plans still de rigueur. The legacy of Dr Ward's discovery was that light was vital if plants were to thrive and so the greenhouse was the ideal environment in which to grow the dozens of bedding plants needed for the elaborate displays that were the fashion.

A new name emerged to answer and advise the middle classes on how to decorate their homes with plants. James Shirley Hibberd lived and gardened in Stoke Newington where he, more than any other writer of this period, wrote from personal experience of growing anything from ferns to potatoes. Although he was not a professional gardener, he wrote with the enthusiasm of a modern television presenter, always looking for the latest gardening innovation and testing new varieties of flowers and vegetables. For many years, he published a magazine, the *Floral World*, full of practical advice and light years away from the scientific botanical journals available as well as the magazines aimed purely at professional gardeners.

His best-known book, *Rustic Adornments for Homes of Taste*, first appeared in 1856, and remains a fascinating reminder of what was considered 'good taste' in middle-class homes of the time. Covering everything from aquariums to apiaries, topics ranged from 'Seaweeds best suited for growth in Aquaria' to 'Suggestions for the formation, at little expense, of Aviaries in dwelling-houses' and 'Can Bees be kept in towns?'[2] In addition, the book focused on 'tasteful' gardening suggestions for the fernery, rockery and wilderness, and flower garden.

Hibberd knew for whom he was writing: the burgeoning middle classes who felt they were just as entitled to feel that their home was their castle as was the prince in his. 'We know already that the luxuries of refinement are no longer monopolized by the great, that the merchant is not rendered sordid by commerce,' he reassured his readers. 'A Home of Taste is a tasteful home, wherein everything is a reflection of refined thoughts and chaste desires.'[3] Hibberd was a great fan of the Wardian case and gave many suitable plant lists in his books.

Alternatives to Nathaniel Ward's miniature greenhouse were quickly produced by rivals. Sir John Robison of Edinburgh reported in Mrs Loudon's magazine that he had built a plant-case for indoor use to which he had 'introduced some essential improvements' which would provide 'the perfect isolation of the air within the case from commixture with the air of the apartment it may be placed in'.[4] Robison's case was recommended by Jane Loudon as a better design than one made by a Mr Ellis, so there was no shortage of variations on Ward's designs. Another idea was Pascall's Patent Propagating Pot from Pascall's West Kent Potteries, which worked on the same principle as Ward's cases. This was a flowerpot with a rim which held a glass dome, an 'ingenious contrivance' according to Hibberd.

Not that Wardian cases and Pascall's pots were the answer to every indoor gardener's prayer: plants enclosed in these miniature glasshouses still needed careful tending, watering and occasional ventilation. How then did the houses of nobility during the London season, puzzled Hibberd, display 'ferns and flowering plants in cases which a few weeks before were a disgrace to the establishment'? Not surprisingly, money provided the answer, with a local nurseryman switching troughs with 'the choicest ferns, and exotic palms and orchises . . . and presto! the Wardian Case "blooms in beauty like the smile of love".'[5]

For thirty years, in the middle of the nineteenth century, middle-class Britain was bewitched by some of the oldest plants in the world: ferns. Charles Kingsley, writing in his essay on natural history, *Glaucus, or the wonders of the shore*, in 1855, showed who was most caught up in this latest horticultural hysteria.

> Your daughters, perhaps, have been seized with the prevailing 'Pteridomania', and are collecting and buying ferns, with Ward's cases wherein to keep them (for which you have to pay), and wrangling over unpronounceable names of species (which seem different in each new Fern-book that they buy), till the Pteridomania seems to be somewhat of a bore: and yet you cannot deny that they find enjoyment in it, and are more active, more cheerful, more self-forgetful over it, than they would have been over novels and gossip, crochet and Berlin-wool.[6]

Kingsley's essay was mainly praising another fad that gripped middle-class families. This was a fascination with all things 'marine' such as seashore finds and shell collecting. In the home, this led to a plethora of aquaria, many of which incorporated plant life as well.

This was not the first time that ferns had caught the public's imagination. In the late eighteenth century, new varieties were brought back to England and they stirred horticultural interest as plants worth growing for their beauty. By 1825, over a hundred exotic varieties, said to rival the collection at Kew, were grown by Conrad Loddiges at his famous Hackney nursery.

But it was a tiny book, *A Handbook of British Ferns*, 'small enough to be carried in lady's reticule', that started the main fern craze in Britain in 1848. An immediate bestseller for the author Thomas Moore, he then produced a second book, *A Popular History of the British Ferns*, which had beautiful coloured plates and was aimed at young amateurs. These two books had many imitators, all of which produced a flurry of would-be fern collectors searching the British countryside for even more beautiful and obscure discoveries. Shirley Hibberd's *The Fern Garden* (1869) is among the best. The development of the Wardian case and its various cousins undoubtedly helped to encourage these collectors to bring their finds home and attempt to grown them on under glass. Failing that, most nurseries now sold a wide variety of hardy and exotic ferns.

But the Victorian love of ferns went further than the Wardian case that had itself become a symbol of Victorian design taste. Ferns were pressed, dried and mounted for display in frames. Fern silhouettes were created by ink splatter work. In the 1860s and 1870s, ferns replaced flowers as the motif of choice on furnishing fabrics, wallpaper and tiles. Garden furniture manufacturers fashioned wrought-iron tables, chairs and benches. But the public are a fickle lot and by the 1880s they had tired of 'pteridology' and had moved on. Its linguistic legacy was more lasting. In 1969, D. E. Allen listed thirty-three words added to the *Oxford English Dictionary* in its wake, including 'fernery', 'fern-mania' and, saddest of all, 'fern robbers' defined as 'ruthless over-collectors of ferns, by implication without real knowledge and for money'.[7]

In addition to elaborate aquaria and fernery displays, there were other ingenious ideas for displaying plants. Annie Hassard, one of several women who wrote gardening books, in her case specifically for 'ladies and amateurs', suggested a fake raised tabletop with a circular hole into which could be displayed young tree ferns or palms. A more practical idea, one that was extremely popular in European countries, was a living plant screen, known as a *zimmerlaube*, to go in front of an empty fire during the summer months. A grandchild of the Georgian bough pots, this was a trough backed with a sheet of trellis the size of the fireplace opening which had variegated ivy intertwined through it, the bare soil planted with the low-growing fern *Selaginella denticulata* with cut blooms of large flowers.

When it came to advising on the arrangement of plants in a room, Hassard took advantage of the confused copyright laws of the time and reproduced a complete chapter from Frederick Burbidge's *Domestic Floriculture*, published in 1874. Burbidge worked for William Robinson's weekly journal *The Garden* after being a star student at the Royal Horticultural Society's Chiswick gardens and at Kew. Later he was to go off plant-hunting himself with Harry Veitch in search of orchids, pitcher plants and ferns for conservatory growing. In addition to his excellent botanical knowledge, Burbidge had strong ideas on how plants should be displayed in the home. Extracts from this chapter paint a vivid picture of what a Victorian parlour might have looked like if Burbidge's readers followed his suggestions.

Zinc pans neatly enamelled or painted may be used in the case of large pots which have to be set down on the floor or carpet. For smaller plants which require elevating near the light, neat

rustic jardinettes or ornamental flower-stands may be used to
excellent effect . . . Brown or varnished wicker-baskets are well
suited as receptacles for pot-plants . . . no matter what receptacles
are employed for pot-plants, they should not be decorated so as to
attract the eye from the plants. A soft neutral brown tint is best,
as it harmonises with the other furniture . . . Ivy grows well in the
shade, and may be employed for trailing around sofas or couches
. . . and rustic picture-frames.[8]

Although the retailers' catalogues were full of them, gardening
writer Miss E. A. Maling, about whom we know little, disapproved
of wire flower stands, which she thought, were impractical. She did
acknowledge that they 'were very nice-looking when freshly filled',
did not take up much room and were easy to move around. Her main
objection to them was that they were hard to make 'look ornamental',
especially since she was a great believer in surrounding pots with damp
moss not just to hide them but to help them retain moisture.

Miss Maling's preference was for zinc-lined wooden stands, rustic in
pattern, varnished for the conservatory or decorated with china tiles,
or of zinc 'ornamented in white and gold' if they were for the drawing-
room. She recommended always measuring the space available before
buying stands, no doubt still smarting from the time she had 'a plant-
case brought home, that to [her] astonishment and dismay, could not,
by any manoeuvring, be got in through the door!'[9]

However, such subtlety in hiding plant containers was rarely seen in
the private home, especially after the Great Exhibition of 1851. It was
here that the British nation (and plenty of foreigners, too) turned out
to see the best that the workshop of the world was producing. Queen
Victoria visited several times and, in all, six million tickets were sold.

During one of the queen's visits she was shown round by Herbert
Minton, one of the original guarantors of the exhibition as well as a
major exhibitor. The exhibition was a turning point for Minton's
Stoke-on-Trent firm. This was where it launched the majolica glazed
ware that was to become the latest 'must-have' for every Victorian
middle-class parlour. Minton was encouraged to revive the encaustic
technique, particularly for tiles by 'the father of the Gothic Revival',
A. W. N. Pugin. Not surprisingly many of the objects reflected this
in their design leitmotif. Heavily encrusted with leaves and flowers
in brightly coloured lead glazes, this was the antithesis of Burbidge's
neutral browns.

Some of the more old-fashioned flowers no longer looked right in these brash containers. 'Our ordinary London Mignonette boxes have given place to late years, to fine majolica troughs, overflowing with the most brilliant blossoms,' wrote a correspondent in *The Garden* in 1873.[10] Some thought this fashion for grouping 'many-coloured flowering plants in many-coloured receptacles' in bad taste. But these designs caught the mood of domestic design at the time, which was heavy – some would say oppressive – highly ornate and above all floral. It was not just enough to have living plants in the home but the jardinières and cachepots were painted and decorated with floral motifs. Flowerpot covers were 'woven' with sprigs of corn, lavender or barley and 'new bright-green satin ribbon'. Plain pots were wreathed in loosely wound fabric or sheathed in pleated paper covers.

There was great competition among manufacturers to produce glass plant-cases based on Ward's theories but with subtle improvements which allowed them to be patented so they could not be copied by the competition. Miss Maling had fallen foul of such legal problems after the publication of the first edition of her book, *In-door Plants and how to grow them, for the drawing-room, balcony, and greenhouse.* When the second edition of this popular little book came out a year later, in 1862, she admitted that she could no longer go into details of the type of case she had had made up for by a carpenter since '[he] is no longer employed by me; *nor is he at liberty to make the cases for others*' (original italics) because, she explained, 'they can only be made by the legally appointed maker, whose name and address will be found at the end of the book.'[11] A deal had obviously been struck with the makers, Pickard and Co. of All Saints' Place, King's Cross. Another supplier was Mr F. W. Ball of Sussex Street in Norwich, who recommended his design which was easy to fix to the outside of a window frame. The selling point was that 'the comfort of the room is increased in winter by its shutting-out the cold, and is cooling in summer'.[12]

While the conservatory had by now come within the reach of many middle-class families, it was not always easy to add one to an existing house. The most desirable setup was to be able to walk from the domestic living area straight into the conservatory but where this was not possible, there were other novel alternatives. Miss Maling wrote that she had heard of 'several places [where] the drawing-room [has] the usual looking-glass frame over the chimney-piece, but filled, instead of looking-glass, with a large plate of transparent glass, giving a full view of the brilliant flowers and hanging baskets of a beautiful conservatory beyond'.[13]

A less drastic alternative if space was short was to build out of the windows. Based on the same scientific assumptions as his original 'Wardian' case, houses were adapted to include a *hortus fenestralis*, 'double windows': windows with built-in glass cabinets for plant growing. One of the few remaining examples can be seen at the Linley Sambourne house in London's Kensington. Frederick Burbidge described what he thought were some of the best window cases he had seen at the City of London Club in Old Broad Street.

Here are four cases, two at each end of a large dining hall: and the plants – which in some cases consist of choice kinds, as Cyathea princips, Todea superba, and the elegant climbing Lygodiums – are remarkable for their fresh and vigorous growth, although in the midst of the London smoke and a dust-laden atmosphere. These window-cases are built outside the plate-glass windows, and are tastefully fitted with rockwork and little pools of clear water, while the charming glimpses of fresh and elegant vegetation thus obtained give a cheerful appearance to the room that could scarcely be obtained by any other means.[14]

Pendant and climbing ferns were also recommended while the British middle classes were obsessed with 'fernmania'. The ever-enthusiastic Shirley Hibberd had plenty of suggestions for planting up such window cases, some for permanent planting, others to be rotated in a series of trays which could be grown on in the greenhouse. Lilies of the valley, auriculas, primulas, violets, myrtle, anemone, mignonette, musk, nemophilus, dwarf ipomeas and common ivy were just some of the plants Hibberd recommended though presumably not all at once. Gesnerias, gloxinias, achimenes, hydrangeas, roses, calceolarias, fuchsias and pansies all, he promised, 'thrive[d] well in a moist atmosphere'.[15] Thankfully, he did point out that pelargoniums and cacti were not suitable for such enclosures.

Another suggestion was that a corner room could be turned over to a 'winter garden' for the display of evergreen stove-plants. Readers were counselled to check first that the room did not face north, 'but where a choice can be made, one should be selected which faces the south, east, or west . . . an excess of solar lighting can be regulated by means of shading, etc., while a deficiency of light cannot be supplied by any means whatever.' Light-coloured wallpaper or paint was also recommended. A distinction was made between 'dwelling-rooms which are generally warmer and more dusty' and 'reception-rooms, the temperature of which in winter averages from 55 deg. to 60 deg. Fahr.' [13–15°C], a reminder of just how cold Victorian houses would seem to us.[16]

There were alternative ideas for those who had no space to build out from their houses. In 1838, J. C. Loudon suggested turning garrets into little greenhouses by training plants out of the windows and on to the roofs. In 1859, an engineer, William Bridges Adam, came up with, at that time, an eccentric idea of converting flat roofs across London into roof gardens. While ignoring most of the obvious practical problems of having plants on a roof in a city with serious smoke pollution, he was convinced that these 'housetop gardens' would improve even the poorest lifestyle. This idea was taken up by *The Garden* magazine:

> It is within the means of any man who builds a good house to have a garden on the roof, which during the summer, can be filled with the most luscious grapes, peaches, plums, etc, and in the winter with plants, the beauty of the flowers of which will afford a charm far beyond the trifling cost of their maintenance.

That had been thought of as well: 'The demand for care-takers would bring forward a host of candidates for this new branch of industry, and it might furnish an excellent and remunerative vocation for women.'[17]

In 1874 an article appeared in *The Garden* magazine describing the 'House-top Garden in the City' belonging to Mr Lascelles, the 'horticultural builder', of Bunhill Row, Finsbury. The rooftop conservatory was on top of Mr Lascelles's offices and *The Garden* found it so inspiring that they thought

> such a pleasant innovation in the city naturally suggests many ways in which a like kind of glasshouse might be made to add to the comfort and elegance of private houses of every class, from those who could afford a well-furnished winter-garden to those who could only use the upper storey as a playground for children.[18]

Mr Lascelles's house-top garden was 'tastefully arranged . . . with choice Ferns, Selaginellas, Begonias, Ficus, and other decorative plants, while more recently, we believe, several species of choice Orchids in hanging-baskets have been added'.[19] However, the idea of gardens on rooftops did not catch on and in spite of their philanthropic desires neither did the idea of communal roof gardens on apartment buildings.

There was no shortage of wisdom and advice on what equipment might be needed to care for a houseful of potted plants. Large tools borrowed from the garden shed were not thought appropriate to indoor work, which was more often than not done by the women of the household. As Frederick Burbidge so generously pointed out, 'In tasteful homes, where there are ladies, the window-gardening may safely be left in their hands; and it is really astonishing what quick progress the dear, nimble-fingered creatures make in this delightful art.'[20]

Miss Maling, herself a pretty 'nimble-fingered creature', recommended that lady gardeners should always wear a pair of gloves which should have 'closed linen gauntlets sewed to them, and with an elastic to keep them up the arm, so that they can be pulled off at once, leaving the sleeves and hands unsoiled'. A small pair of scissors were thought useful together with a 'very small syringe, or a little, sharpish brush such as is used for dusting picture-frames', something no Victorian home would have been without. Completing the list was a steel trowel, a sharp penknife, a wide-mouth bottle (for collecting cuttings), a small 'watering-pot' with a long spout and a watertight rose that screwed on, a couple of yards of 'common brown calico for soaking up . . . any over-splashing of water', together with a 'common mahogany tray' on which to keep everything.[21]

Pest control was also considered. One of the advantages of Wardian or close cases, claimed Burbidge, was that the plants were seldom infested by insects. For other plants this was not the case, and even in these pre-central heating days, greenfly and red spider mite could be troublesome. Burbidge gave a recipe for a sponging solution for plants, which involved boiling an ounce (30 g) of quassia chips in three pints of soft water and then allowing it to cool. A less environmentally friendly suggestion was that if there were only a few greenfly, 'the fumes from a pipe or cigar will soon settle them, care being taken not to burn the plant in the operation'. Who needed a separate smoking room when a husband's nightly cigar might do so much good to the plants!

More serious infestations could be treated with any of a number of new chemical treatments that were becoming available from firms such as 'Fowler's' or 'Frettingham's'. Miss Maling was a fan of 'Dumont's Insect Powder', which was sold, she told her readers, 'in little gutta-percha balls'. The technique was to squeeze the ball so that the powder thickly dusted the plant, after which Miss Maling said she could 'promise a perfect clearance of the insects within three or four hours after the application'.[22]

In spite of all the problems associated with growing healthy plants, the mid-nineteenth century was a horticultural high point in the home. This was a curious contradiction considering how unsuitable many middle-class homes were for growing plants. But a combination of botanical excitement and technical innovation meant that this will forever be remembered as the time when plants in the home were a source of pride and accomplishment.

CHAPTER 10

GARDENS UNDER GLASS

<blockquote>

etween the conservatory and the greenhouse there is about the same difference as between a dinner and a luncheon . . . The greenhouse is intended principally for production . . . The conservatory is intended for enjoyment and display . . . the free movement of full-grown persons attired in a manner which would render it inconvenient for them to come in contact with damp flower-pots. A conservatory should be more or less a garden under glass, and adapted for frequent resort and agreeable assemblage at all seasons, and especially at times of festivity.[1]

</blockquote>

Shirley Hibberd's description of the perfect Victorian conservatory, with its images of ladies in heavy velvet skirts sweeping along tiled paths brushing past luxuriant tree ferns and stooping to smell the scent of a rare orchid, fits with the artistic representations we have of these 'gardens under glass' such as those by Tissot and Manet.

In its literary mythology, the conservatory has become a place of assignation, somewhere with a different feel to the rest of the house although it was often joined to it. It is a place where heroines met their lovers under the pretext of plant care. The description of a fictional conservatory in Charlotte Yonge's novel of 1856, *The Daisy Chain, or Aspirations*, captures this sentiment completely: 'It's a real bower for a maiden of romance, with its rich green fragrance in the midst of winter. It is like a picture in a dream. One could imagine it as a fairy land, where no care, or grief, or weariness could come.'[2]

The reality was not such a fairyland, however, and the best displays certainly required plenty of care and no doubt some grief and weariness as well. As another young heroine of Charlotte Yonge's realized, to be able to have 'a garden with a hothouse like Mr Brown's' involved having lots of money.[3] Indeed it did; in the country homes of the upper classes, armies of gardeners were employed to tend a vast range of exotic flowers and fruit. A whole range of hot-houses would have been aspired to: not just for plants but also to produce flowers for the house and out-of-season fruit. 'One wonders how a Duke could live without peaches and grapes, not to say pine-apples, forced strawberries, and kidneybeans,' questioned the *Gardener's Magazine*.[4] The answer is they did not. Most would have had all these and camellia, orchid and fern houses complete with aquaria and aviaries on a scale that rivalled public displays.

The less wealthy could visit some superb conservatories which opened to the public. These 'winter gardens' were an idea imported from the Continent. They soon became a popular weekend destination for family outings. When Paxton's Crystal Palace was safely moved and reassembled in South London, part of the structure was given over to a 'winter garden' containing orange trees and pomegranates once belonging to King Louis-Philippe of France. In Regent's Park, the Royal Botanic Society's Winter Garden opened to the public in 1846, and was immediately captivating.

> From the keen, frosty air outside, and flowerless aspect of universal nature, one steps into an atmosphere balmy and delicious and not in the slightest degree oppressive. The most exquisite odours are wafted to and fro with every movement of the glass doors. Birds singing in the branches . . . make you again and again pause to ask, is this winter? Is this England?[5]

It must have been a treat to visit.

The upper classes were able to capture that feeling of exoticism and 'other worldiness' in their own large glasshouses. The 6th Earl of Harrowby remembered as a small boy his mother entertaining her friends in the conservatory at the family home of Sandon Hall in Staffordshire.

> My mother and the other ladies dressed for it as if they were in the tropics, in long spotted muslins with flowing ribbons. The conservatory was kept so hot because it was full of exotic plants, strong scented crotons, beautiful colour tropical flowers (no camellias then, it was too hot), bananas and oranges (though these only fruit occasionally) and palms.[6]

But among the majority of middle-class homes, such elegance could only be dreamed of – and many did – trying to turn their dreams into reality with mixed degrees of success. The conservatory was seen as an indoor garden, somewhere exotic plants could be grown and displayed without any of the problems of lack of light or the crippling effects of gas fumes or coal soot. It was also somewhere for the women of the house to focus on, particularly during the winter months. Maintaining this sort of display was labour intensive but that was something that the Victorian middle-class home was never short of whether from family members or household servants.

By the mid-nineteenth century, conservatories were frequently added to houses as a piece of one-upmanship. Sadly, they were rarely suitable for serious display and their owners often took the easiest option when it came to planting. William Robinson (1838–1935), writing on Parisian gardening, was critical of English conservatories: 'We build more glass houses than any other nation, but have as yet nearly everything to learn as to the arrangement of the most important of them, or what is usually called the conservatory.'[7] Shirley Hibberd also had no patience with gardeners who were not prepared to be adventurous in their choice of plants either through laziness or the desire to specialize.

It is simply a tax on one's patience . . . to pass from a blaze of geraniums in the parterre to another blaze of geraniums in the conservatory . . . a rabbit cooked a hundred different ways is tiresome, and the cooking must be very tiresome to the rabbit.[8]

Many indoor gardeners did want more of a challenge than just growing pelargoniums. Planting schemes came in and out of vogue so it is often possible to date illustrations of conservatories to within 20 years or so. In the early nineteenth century, J. C. Loudon had advised conservatory owners to stick to the tried-and-tested plants bordering on hardiness such as citrus and camellias. The sudden influx of tropical plants towards the middle of the century encouraged those with the know-how or money to use the conservatory as a display room for a whole range of new species. The 1840s saw the peak of exotic planting, much on white staging with little attempt to be anything other than a botanical show. However, by the mid-century it became fashionable to transform the conservatory into the horticultural fairyland of Charlotte Yonge's book. Out went the white staging and in came elaborate and theatrical displays of plants designed to create the effect of a miniature winter garden attached to the home.

There was no shortage of advice – and criticism – for the new middle-class conservatory gardener on how to achieve this effect. These 'small glass rooms without any provision for heating . . . are very often ill-ventilated and rather dark', noted T. C. March, head gardener to the Duke of Grafton, in 1862.[9] His suggestion for such conservatories was to order a quarter of a ton of Derbyshire 'tufa', a grey porous limestone, to be heaped up on the presumably strong wooden staging and then dressed with mosses and ferns that would cling to the limestone.

There followed a list of plants that 'with a little contrivance' could be tucked between the tufa 'so that all [they] appear to spring from amongst the rocks'. These included 'the Arum, the Indian-rubber tree, and, above all, the Mimosa, which is admirably adapted for these houses, and looks like a small palm tree'. Azaleas, camellias or cinerarias, Chinese primroses, ferns, bulbs of all sorts, primroses, saxifrage, moss, ivy and periwinkle were also suggested. 'Good moss' was hard to come by at markets, noted Mr March, who recommended that a better plan was 'to write to some country friend to send up a good hamper occasionally from the nearest wood'![10] Miss Maling was less dismissive and said that 'luxuriant specimens' of moss could be easily obtained from the men who sell primroses in the streets. Together with a succession of pot-grown bulbs, this display would 'prove more interesting than merely placing the required number of pots in regular file upon wooden shelves', noted Mr March.[11]

In spite of the introduction of basic heating methods, by the 1860s, in middle-class homes at least, there was a move away from the tropical exotics that required an uncomfortable amount of heat and humidity so close to the living rooms. This was in addition to the expense of setting up the conservatory and maintaining the correct temperatures by the opening and closing of shutters and blinds throughout the day. The majority of conservatory owners needed little encouragement to cram these extra rooms to bursting with potted plants.

Although many were hardy, this did not necessarily mean a less elaborate planting plan. Shirley Hibberd described with glee the 'rustic plant-house' combining a conservatory, a smoking room and an outdoor vertical rockery in one extension a neighbour of his, J. T. Pickburn Esq., had added to his house in Stoke Newington.

The walls consisted of a large body of earth enclosed between two facings of brickwork, the outside consisting of rough "burrs" such as are commonly employed for rockeries . . . the whole of these rough walls are planted with ferns, ivies, and hardy succulents . . . The entrance to [the plant-house] from the smoking-room is fantastically decorated with "virgin cork" . . . The roof is furnished with a number of elegant baskets, well filled with showy plants of suitable character, and the walk is terminated by a fountain, at the back of which is placed a number of pieces of looking-glass, which reflect and re-reflect the splashing of the water.[12]

Mr Pickburn was no doubt the envy of all his neighbours. Throughout the Victorian period, the well-filled conservatory remained the pinnacle of domestic status symbols. In addition to the displays of ferns in Wardian cases that graced so many parlours and windows, displays in conservatories gave collectors the opportunity to show off not just a much wider range of plants but also much larger specimens as well. A basic planting of ferns, palms, crotons and coleus was supplemented by a steady supply of flowering pot plants sunk into the beds and replaced as necessary.

Coleus (*Solenostemon scutellarioides*) was extremely popular. Closely related to plectranthus, the earliest plants, *C. fruticosus* (*P. fruticosus*), arrived from the Cape of Good Hope area in South Africa in 1774. Tough and fragrant, coleus was quickly adopted as a window plant, as Shirley Hibberd reported, 'of the artizan's window, and the plant most frequently seen of any at cottagers' and window gardeners' exhibitions'.[13]

In the 1860s coleus fever grabbed the English gardener. In 1861, the *Gardeners' Chronicle* reported that a new coleus from Java, *C. verschaffeltii*, had been shown at the Royal Horticultural Society's Grand Fruit and Flower Show in June that year, 'a plant like the common coleus, but the leaves almost wholly empurpled'. It quickly reported back, recommending gardeners to try growing it since 'this is a first rate plant of its kind I think all will admit who have seen it grown.' Introduced by William Bull's King's Road nursery, its foliage was described as 'elegant in shape, and on the young plants deep crimson, margined with bright green, but as the plants attain age and size the green passes away, and the entire leaf is a rich glowing crimson'.[14]

Rival nursery Veitch's were also scouring the world for plants and their second coleus discovery, which they named *C. veitchii*, 'had almost heart-shaped leaves of a deep chocolate colour, with the edges a bright lively green'.[15] At Chiswick, RHS hybridist Mr F. Bause worked on four varieties that were brought back with astounding results. In 1868, twelve new hybrid plants were auctioned by the RHS and raised the incredible amount of £390. The Veitch nursery bought six plants, including a variety named after its grower, *C. bauseii*, for which they paid 59 guineas. Plants were quickly advertised selling at between 10*s.* 6*d.* and 15*s.* each in the *Gardeners' Chronicle*.

Within a few months, William Bull retaliated with another advertisement. 'If the public is not to be sated with new coleuses, there is now a *bonne bouche* in store for it in the shape of a group of splendid crimson and gold varieties, which have been raised at Chiswick during the past summer.'[16] Sadly for Mr Bull, he had missed his chance as seed was now offered and the sale of his hybrids only raised a total of 65 guineas.

A little surprisingly, Shirley Hibberd was not such a great fan of the coleus family. In 1869, he reported that 'the horticultural world may be said to be in a Coleus fever.' Of the three varieties that he chose to illustrate, *C. marshalli, C. murrayi* and *C. telfordi aurea*, he claimed they 'represent fashionable weeds, beautiful, useful, interesting; nevertheless, weeds which in a few years hence will probably be utterly valueless, and perhaps unknown'. Hibberd was right. Perhaps it was their lack of a horticultural challenge that put him off. Despite having seen specimen pyramids of *C. verschaffeltii* growing in conservatories 9 feet (2.75 m) high and as much at the base, his tone was dismissive when he commented, 'to grow such plants requires only steady attention; skill is almost out of the question.'[17]

For Londoners wishing to pick and choose what they wanted for their own conservatories, there were several large nurseries with a wide range of tender plants of which Veitch's Exotic Nursery remained the most famous. There is not the space here to list the number of introductions that were made through this nursery's pioneering sponsorship of plant hunters. In addition to the thousands of hardy shrubs and trees discovered across the world, there were other smaller but just as significant introductions such as the scented *Calceolaria alba*, which came from Chile in the early 1840s and became the first of the family so beloved as a flowering pot plant by Victorians.

A trip round the Veitch nurseries was like visiting a horticultural wonderland: among greenhouses filled with camellias and orchids, orange trees were rarities such as *Streptocarpus biflorus* and the tropical climber *Thunbergia mysorensis*. Thomas Lobb had found *Hoya lanceolata* subsp. *bella* in Burma, which the *Botanical Magazine* later described as 'the most lovely of all hoyas, resembling an amethyst set in silver'.[18] Plant hunting was often a dangerous business. Gottlieb Zahn, working for James Veitch Jr, drowned while plant hunting in Costa Rica. He is commemorated in *Guzmania zahnii*, a popular bromeliaceous plant with scarlet bracts.

Veitch's nursery was a 'mecca for gardeners . . . a vast and complex ship steaming . . . a liner of class, of taste, even beauty'.[19] John Gould Veitch, the scion of the Veitch family, was an inveterate plant collector. In addition to finding *Pandanus veitchii*, one of the most popular indoor or 'stove' plants of the Victorian period, he introduced twenty-three different kinds of crotons as well as varieties of dracaena and coleus still commonly grown as houseplants. The nursery itself housed offices, a seed warehouse, a library and a herbarium. 'Show Rooms' were available for important visitors, royalty and botanists. All staff who had contact with customers wore frock coats and white gloves.

One of Veitch's many specialities was the begonia. In 1688, Hans Sloane had found a plant that was later identified as belonging to the begonia family, similar to plants discovered in Mexico in the mid-seventeenth century. There are now over 1,000 species in the family Begoniaceae, named by Charles Plumier, the Jesuit missionary and plant collector in 1690 for Michael Begon, governor of Santo Domingo, in what is now the Dominican Republic.

Begonias arrived in European gardens in the late eighteenth century, and by 1815 the Botanic Gardens at Kew were growing eight species, including what was called *B. nitida* (now *B. minor*), the first begonia to flower in Europe. By 1829, fifteen varieties were available to grow in English gardens and that number quickly grew as a flood of new introductions arrived, particularly spurred on by the efforts of the Veitch nursery. *B. coccinea* was discovered by William Lobb in Brazil, and introduced by the Veitch nursery in their catalogue in 1842.

B. rex reputedly came from Assam in 1856 and was one of many ornamental-leaved varieties that were so popular in Victorian parlours because of their toughness and tolerance of low light levels. *B. daedalea*, which arrived from Mexico in 1861, was prized for its young pink-red leaves and leaf stalks richly tinted with carmine. Shirley Hibberd, a great lover of begonias, reported in 1870 that it was described in France as 'la perle, le bijou de tous les Begonias passés, présents, nous oserions presque dire, futurs' [the pearl, the jewel of all begonias past, present, we dare almost to say, and future].[20]

In 1865, *B. boliviensis* was found by Richard Pearce, another Veitch collector; it was the first tuberous begonia to be brought back to Britain. Pearce was also responsible for finding *B. veitchii*, *B. davisii*, and the only species with yellow flowers, which was named after him, *B. pearcei*.

As happened to so many plant hunters of the nineteenth century, he did not grow old enjoying his discoveries, as Shirley Hibberd explained:

In the summer of 1868 [Pearce] started from England to make collections in South America for Mr William Bull, of the King's Road, Chelsea. He arrived at Panama on the 7th. of July, was taken ill on the 13th., and died on the 19th., the malady which caused his death being a fever peculiar to the marshy district in which he commenced his new search for botanical treasure. During the nine years previously he had been abroad collecting plants, and throughout the whole of that period had corresponded with a lady in England to whom he was deeply attached. On his return from Peru, after the journey in which he discovered *B. falcifolia* and many more valuable plants, he married the object of his affections, and soon after set out again on the adventure which cost him his life – a melancholy end to a career which until then was as bright with future promise, as it was already lustrous with achievements beneficial to mankind . . . It is well we should sometimes meditate on the enormous cost at which many of our most cherished enjoyments have been obtained for us.[21]

By 1882, Veitch's were the largest and most influential nursery in the country but they were not without their competitors. Wills & Segar, 'florists, floral decorators, palm growers', were based at the Royal Exotic Nursery and Floral Establishment in Onslow Crescent in Knightsbridge not far from the former site of the Great Exhibition. As at Veitch's, a visit to the nursery must have been an exhilarating experience: a uniformed doorman greeted each customer as they arrived at the entrance to the nursery. This opened out into a large 'winter garden', full of display palms and exotics to whet the appetite. They might then be escorted around the greenhouses by one of the heads of the various different departments, resplendent in frock coat and top hat. There they might choose from forty-two varieties of Selaginella mosses or eighty-six varieties of crotons (now codiæum) ranging in price from 2*s*. 6*d*. to 63*s*. for *C. latimaculatus*, a prized new introduction. Once the selection was made, the plants were delivered by one of six horse-drawn vans that Wills & Segar kept in their nearby stables.

A large part of their business was supplying cut flowers from two other nurseries that they owned, one in Fulham and one in south-east London. By 1875, the company had two Royal Warrants, one for supplying Queen Victoria, and one from the Prince and Princess of Wales. The word 'florist' had almost lost its original connotation of the specialist plant fancier, and in the nineteenth century was moving towards its modern meaning of a person in the business of selling and arranging cut flowers. At this stage it could still also mean 'those who deal chiefly in exotics or greenhouse plants to be sold in pots'.[22]

For those who found the likes of Veitch's and Wills & Segar too intimidating and expensive, there was still Covent Garden. In 1872, it had expanded with the opening of a separate flower market. Flowering pot plants were sold at the crack of dawn to hawkers who then wheeled them on barrows around the London streets. A wide variety of plant stock and conservatory accessories were also sold to the public from indoor shops at the market that were supplied by small independent nurseries. Of the tasteful containers so admired by Miss Maling, the rustic tubs with intertwining artificial ivy were available from 7s. to 20s. each at the Bedford Conservatory, 'above the central avenue of Covent-garden market' and also across south London. They won the approval of gardener and author T. C. March, who said 'they [were] always in good taste, and never leave the least impression of a cockney paradise.'[23]

Stalls at Covent Garden were supplied by rapidly expanding wholesale market garden nurseries. Whereas in 1871 there were only active thirty plant stalls, by 1891 this had mushroomed to 300 growers. That year, 20,000 vanloads of plants were delivered to the market. One of the most successful suppliers was a nursery started by the Rochford family, Michael and his sons, Thomas and John. Michael Rochford originally specialized in grapes but as imports brought prices down, he began growing plants for the home, devoting several greenhouses just to *Ficus elastica*, the India-rubber plant. Beneath their broad, oval leaves were pots of *Selaginella denticulata*, popular to cover bare soil in pots. There were three houses just for the Delta maidenhair fern (*Adiantum raddianum*).

Thomas, Michael Rochford's son, had started his own nursery first in Tottenham and then on the Turnford Hall estate in Hertfordshire in 1884. In addition to having eleven acres devoted to hothouse plants – ferns, orchids and lilies in particular – he became famous for his skill at chilling hundreds and thousands of lily of the valley crowns (*Convallaria majalis*), thus extending the season of this highly popular plant. Over 100 Rochford greenhouses contained palms including the wild date palm (*Phoenix rupicola*), which, it was said, could 'hardly be beaten for drawing-room decoration'.[24]

Outside London, provincial companies also flourished. Cheltenham had three florist shops that also supplied pot plants. Two of the smaller shops, owned by a Miss Holder and a Mr Phillips respectively, had busy businesses hiring plants out during the town's social 'season'. The largest business, however, was run by a former head gardener, James Cypher, who started his own Exotic Nursery in the early 1860s. Cypher specialized in dramatic decorations and supplied window boxes, palms and window grottoes stuffed with exotic plants and statuary. He also entered competitions, which he nearly always won, transporting large potted palms and other plants in a horse-drawn caravan as far away as Manchester.

It is more than likely that the palms that James Cypher was transporting across the country were the relatively newly discovery, the Kentias (*Howea forsteriana*) from Lord Howe Island, 500 miles off the eastern coast of Australia's New South Wales. The island was discovered in 1788 but was not settled until fifty years later. Just under forty years after that, German botanist and plant hunter Ferdinand Mueller first described the palm that was brought back from Lord Howe Island by Charles Moore in 1869. Mueller named it after Kentia, the capital city of Lord Howe Island, while 'forsteriana' was in honour of William Forster, a senator and one-time premier of New South Wales. First classified as *Kentia forsteriana*, it was later renamed *Howea forsteriana* as the genus grew with further discoveries of related species.

This palm happily transferred from the subtropical climate of this Pacific island to the drawing rooms and parlours of Britain without a murmur. It appeared to thrive on neglect, underwatering, coping with anything the English interior could inflict on it. How different to the other palms suggested in the handbooks of Hibberd and others, which required warm, moist atmospheres that could only be accommodated in conservatory conditions.

There was only one other plant that could cope with the darkness and polluted atmosphere of Victorian homes even better than the Kentia palm and that was the aspidistra. By 1865, three varieties of this strange plant were grown in Britain, all having been discovered in China and Japan. The appropriately named Mr John Bull brought over *Aspidistra punctata* from the Happy Valley near Hong Kong in 1863 to Chelsea, which was the centre for aspidistra cultivation at this time. The plant quickly earned its common name of the 'Cast-Iron Plant' because it was soon obvious that it was one of the few indoor plants that could cope with the fumes from the 'Iron-clad' and 'Veritas' patent incandescent mantles and the seemingly inescapable coal gas.

Just as these two stalwarts became firmly installed across Britain, the look of conservatories, drawing rooms and parlours altered. Perhaps disheartened by so many failures, the late Victorians lost their early enthusiasm for horticultural fantasies such as Wardian cases and indoor aquaria. Fewer but larger reliable plants, such as palms, were used in displays. Tastes in interior decoration were also changing. William Morris, who had started his firm of Morris, Marshall, Faulkner and Company in 1861, began to influence trends and ideas through his loathing of high Victorian clutter and commercialism. 'Never have anything in your home that you do not know to be useful, or believe to be beautiful' was the mantra of the Arts and Crafts movement. The violent colours and seed-catalogue perfection of floral wallpapers and furnishing materials in the 1860s were a world away from the classic William Morris designs that have survived and are still popular in the twenty-first century.

By the 1890s, it was not just palms that were ubiquitous but also the palm-leaf fan, which was a popular Aesthetic movement interior accessory. Dried flower arrangements and pampas grass heads were the other obligatory accessories for the artistic salon. Against these 'statement' displays, elaborately planted Wardian cases, artificial indoor rockeries with banks of ferns, however exotic, began to look fussy and dated. While the extremely wealthy continued to spend tens of thousands of pounds on extravagant hot-houses and employing dozens of staff to maintain them, for the average home, as the end of the century approached, it was clear that the love affair with elaborate horticultural displays was on the wane.

CHAPTER 11

WINDOW GARDENS
FOR THE PEOPLE

I f there is one plant that sums up the attitude of Victorian sentimentalists towards the unfortunate working class in the nineteenth century, it is the forlorn red 'geranium' sitting on a cottage windowsill. Hundreds of artists used this as a symbol of aspiring respectability. It was, after all, cheap to obtain ffrom street markets and hard to kill even in the most neglected home. The suggestion was that in these grim, industrial times, there was nothing grown between this and the lush greenery of the middle-class ferneries and the hot-houses of the aristocracy.

For many, the images of the hard life of the nineteenth-century poor come from the works of Charles Dickens, who tried to change the iniquities and inequalities of the society of the time through his writing. Dickens frequently used the garden as a symbol of happily, family-centred homes, plants to represent respectability, and a lack of both to show a person's miserable state. This was never more obvious than in his description of a prisoner's wife in the debtor's prison in *Pickwick Papers*.

> There was a lean and haggard woman . . . who was watering, with great solicitude, the wretched stump of a dried-up withered plant, which, it was plain to see, could never send forth a green leaf again; – too true an emblem, perhaps, of the office she had come there to discharge.[1]

Apart from references to humble homes having plants on the kitchen windowsill to keep flies away from the food, it is hard to pinpoint lower- or working-class involvement in horticulture before the nineteenth century except in the obvious professions of gardeners and nurserymen, and as owners of small country plots used mainly for growing subsistence vegetables. By the nineteenth century, the image of the 'cottage' garden was a romantic one, a patch of land full of a jumble of simple flowers and herbs, many grown 'for the pot'. There was no semblance of 'design' in the classic sense of the word. With the mass move towards city living, which included the swallowing up of land previously used for horticulture of some sort, growing plants became a luxury for those who could afford it, and that was assumed not to be the working man.

In July 1878 the *Yorkshire Post* reported on a local flower show, just what one might expect from a regional newspaper. But this was a rather different flower show, as the flowers were grown under 'various and difficult circumstances'.

> The flower boxes . . . in many instances were soap and powder blue boxes, were ranged in tiers round the spacious room . . . the cleanly appearance and get-up of many a sturdy son of toil, attended by their pale-faced anxious-looking wives, and the gleam of joy that passed over their care-lined faces, was a sight once seen not easily to be forgotten when they bore down on the well-remembered geranium or fuchsia that had been the light of their pent-up home in the midst of smoke and gloom . . . and had come to the fore a prize-winner.[2]

The exhibitors were from a local 'board' school in Leeds, the children of factory workers with little access to green space let alone the facilities of a conservatory, greenhouse or even a garden shed in which to grow plants. Yet these children had produced window boxes, hanging baskets and flowerpots planted up with flowers grown by themselves in their own homes. 'Plants raised in hot houses, or purchased *after growth*, [were] rigidly excluded.' A professional gardener judged the exhibits and there were extra prizes for the 'best box or pot of mignonette, the best box or pot of musk, best arrangement of climbing plants, [and the] best hanging pot or basket of plants'.[3]

The competition was organized by Catherine Buckton, a Unitarian and the wife of Joseph Buckton, who was a wool merchant and manufacturer. In traditional Victorian style, Mrs Buckton involved herself in good works and philanthropic ventures. She was a founder member of the Leeds Ladies Educational Association and of the Yorkshire School of Cookery.

Belying the popular belief that all middle-class women remained exclusively in the private 'sphere' of the home, Buckton also sat on the Leeds School Board and was a popular lecturer to children and pupil-teachers. Several courses of her lectures were turned into books including *Town and Window Gardening*, which came out in 1879. It was dedicated to the memory of Lady Augusta Stanley, who, Buckton said, 'did so much to brighten the homes of the poor in Westminster and to inspire little children with a love of flowers'.[4] A section of the book had originally been published as a pamphlet which was given out to the sixty children who regularly attended Mrs Buckton's lectures 'for a whole year', and who presumably were the competitors in the Leeds flower show.

Rather than preach at them (though she may have done that as well), Mrs Buckton gave them sensible, practical advice on which plants to try and grow, always bearing in mind their home situation and low income. Cowslips, primroses, snowdrops and violets would not grow in 'Smoky Towns', she cautioned. Carrot tops could be grown into foliage plants having been wrapped in moss and placed in a saucer of wet sand. Suitable containers for window gardening could be had from any grocer's shop 'for a few pence . . . round cheese-boxes, powder-blue boxes, fancy soap-boxes . . . look pretty painted green'.[5]

Mrs Buckton also told them she had seen crushed cockleshells used at Kew for drainage, hoping that one day all her students might get the chance to visit the Botanical Gardens. She talked of simple wire hanging baskets and pots displayed under a skylight at the top of the stairs of St Andrew's Chambers in Leeds, where moss and ferns 'gathered in neighbouring wood' thrived. And to tempt her pupils further, she mentioned knowing 'a lady who lives in London [who] has some small-leaved Ivy growing round a wooden picture-frame in her drawing-room. The Ivy is planted in a little wooden trough under the frame, in which flowers are growing.'[6]

In London there were thousands of children whose living conditions were just as bad if not worse than those Leeds board school children. Just as the building boom of the mid-nineteenth century affected the lives of hundreds of thousands of middle-class Britons, so the growth of the industrial cities of the North and Midlands and the capital itself, always a Mecca for those looking for work, changed the lives of millions of working-class Britons – and rarely for the better. By the middle of the century, a third more people were living in cities than had been at the start of it. For many this meant living in appalling conditions of tenements, slums and 'rookeries'. Some would have grown up in the country with memories of green fields and cottage gardens. But time would have dimmed the memory and those born in the cities would have little experience of any greenery, let alone the opportunity or space to grow anything satisfactorily.

If the caring of houseplants appeared to be a uniquely middle-class experience, that is no thanks to the efforts of Catherine Buckton and the Reverend Samuel Hadden Parkes, senior curate of the parish of St George's in London's Bloomsbury. Revd Parkes also saw window and indoor gardening as an opportunity to improve the lives of some of his parishioners in nearby Little Coram Street where housing was 'unhealthy and dilapidated . . . and in some instances there are families residing in both the front and back cellar or kitchen'. These were people 'who generally obtain their living by selling watercresses, fruit, and small toys in the street'. What surprised him, however, was 'the care and attention which some of them bestowed upon a few window plants during the summer'.[7]

A description of what might have been seen by Revd Parkes appeared in an evangelical magazine in 1865.

It is observable that even in the low courts and mews where the roughest costermongers and street Irish congregate, scarcely a window is without its pot or its bower of flowers. We say 'bower', because many of these windows are actually darkened by Virginia creepers, nasturtiums, the pretty yellow 'canariensis', and even common scarlet-runners (these last much affected by stablemen and weavers). A favourite fashion is to surround the ledge of the windows – more especially in stable mews – with tiny green palisades, joined by little miniature imitations of five-barred gates painted white. Within these palisades, and along the ledge, are set pots of any cheap and favourite flowers. Oftentimes a large box is filled with mould [soil], and deep set with common red tulips in spring, mignonette in summer, and marigolds and chrysanthemums in autumn.[8]

Parkes's idea was to organize a flower show in which local poor families would be supplied with plants, which they had to look after for several weeks before returning them for judging in the local Bible Mission Room by a professional horticulturalist. This would, he believed, have a five-fold benefit for his parishioners. First, it would prove that no matter how poor one was, you could have a love of plants. Caring for the plants would give these people a 'simple recreation', he suggested, and in doing so, make them aware how important hygiene was in the home. The plants themselves would have a cleansing effect on the air of these slum rooms, he reasoned. Finally, being an archetypal

Victorian moralist, Revd Parkes also delighted in thinking that the cultivation of these plants might have 'a direct or indirect' influence on their 'spiritual condition', in other words bring them closer to godliness.

In the first year the competition was held in this notoriously poor section of central London; the lure of cash prizes of up to 10s. drew an entry of ninety-four exhibitors. There were three classes: Fathers and Mothers not Flower Dealers, Flower Dealers, and Children. Old cracked teapots 'of the most approved antique pattern, which doubtless years before had brewed the refreshing Bohea in the drawing-rooms of the neighbouring squares' and 'jugs with dilapidated noses ... quasi-flower-pots either freshly raddled or tastefully adorned with old scraps of gaily colour paper-hanging' housed the hopeful entrants' exhibits.[9]

The show was such a success that by the next year exhibitors now included a section for domestic servants, and another for those living 'elsewhere' since it was not considered fair that locals should compete against those with a 'more airy situation and higher social position'. Entries were also divided into sections for fuchsias, geraniums and annuals. A review of the show held in 1864 in the *Gardeners' Chronicle* shows just what a variety of plants were grown in central London slums at that time, and the ingenuity of their owners for devising containers. Today's recyclers would be proud of them.

> The bulk of the plants exhibited consisted of Pelargoniums and Fuchsias; but we also noticed examples of Creeping Jenny, Yellow Calceolaria, white and crimson Pinks, Petunias, Hydrangeas, Dahlias, Verbenas, what are called Nettle Geraniums, Kalosanthes, Orange trees, Balsams, Mignonette, Musk, Asters, and French and African Marigolds ... We ... observed a little round tub filled with Potatoes, Radishes, and a tuft or two of Virginian stock; a sprig of Yew, kept alive some three years in a clear glass bottle, from a nurse in a workhouse; boxfuls of Ferns, and even shells filled with same favourite tribe of plants; hanging baskets made of three-deep Strawberry punnets fastened together ... hanging wire baskets supporting finely bloomed plants of blue lobelia.[10]

Not surprisingly, the Revd Parkes declared the shows an unmitigated success, quoting a widow who lived in a 'back cellar into which the sunshine only came for one hour during the day'. 'I never thought before that a flower would flourish in my room,' she confided to the curate. 'I did not believe before that I should care for anything again in this work like I have cared for that geranium. Indeed, sir, I've got almost to love it as if it could speak.'[11]

Another poor man, reported Parkes,

into whose room the sunshine never comes, with a zeal and energy worthy of all praise, made an ambitious attempt at a conservatory by means of an old orange box and a second hand window sash, which he nailed against the wall of the back yard of the premises in which he lived, and exhibited some very creditable specimens of plants grown under difficulties.[12]

Parkes wrote of his experiences in *Window Gardens for the People, and clean and tidy rooms being an experiment to improve the homes of the London Poor.* Such sentimentalism struck a cord with Victorian Londoners and Parkes's idea was soon tried out in different parts of London. Lady Augusta Stanley (to whom Catherine Buckton had dedicated her book), wife of Dean Stanley, led the movement in Westminster. In the East End, the clergyman responsible for starting similar shows raised funds by writing to *The Times*. In July 1866, he was able to report that his campaign had been supported with £5 from no less a luminary than Florence Nightingale, 'a helpless invalid, herself dependent on window gardening for almost her only pleasure'.[13]

Within the professional horticultural world, however, this sort of show was definitely seen as something not to be taken too seriously. 'This is a social and domestic movement,' reported the *Gardener's Magazine* rather disparagingly, '. . . the horticulturalist can assist only when the clergy and philanthropists associated with them have made a beginning.'[14]

Yet this was also a time that saw the revival of the florists' societies, groups of men dedicated to growing one particular flower to the peak of its perfection. Across the North of England and the Midlands, shows for auriculas, tulips, ranunculus, pinks and carnations were enormously popular. In 1829, the Norfolk and Norwich Horticultural Society were also showing daffodils, dahlias, roses and chrysanthemums. Drawing entries from 'florists and cottagers', these competitions were for working men who could win a silver spoon for their efforts: 'many an industrious, skilful man may furnish himself with a set of silver tea spoons . . . and eat his peas with a handsome silver dessert spoon instead of a pewter or an iron ladle.'[15]

Records of smaller shows elsewhere were rarely kept since few members could 'write or read writing'. But the larger shows became enormously popular, with special classes for 'cottagers' who did not have access to heated greenhouses and had to use makeshift frames and blankets to protect their precious plants from frost.

Ruth Duthie, writing on florists' society, has said that 'the years between 1820 and 1860 saw the artisan florists' movement at its height.'[16] The eight traditional florists' flowers, the auricula, the tulip, the carnation, the polyanthus, the hyacinth, the anemone, the ranunculus, and the pink, were joined in the mid-nineteenth century by the pansy, the dahlia and the chrysanthemum, the last two destined to overtake all the others in popularity for the working man to grow competitively. There was therefore a long traditional of showing among the working classes, apart from the philanthropic efforts of Revd Parkes and Mrs Buckton. As Parkes himself pointed out, 'the fondness with which the poor have ever cultivated flowers in their dismal, dark, dirty rooms, long before any such incitement or encouragement as a flower show was thought of, is very instructive.'[17]

In contrast to the 'Window Gardening for the Poor' movement started by Revd Parkes, many local flower shows were run by their working-class exhibitors for themselves with no altruistic motive other than to show off their prized blooms. This was certainly the case of the Floricultural Society shows held in the East End of London in the 1860s and 1870s.

This was an area that had suffered rapid development earlier in the century as land previously used by nurserymen was swept away for housing. Areas such as Mile End, Bethnal Green, Hackney, Poplar and Old Ford had, in the eighteenth century, 'boasted tulip beds by hundreds'.[18] But by 1866, the *East London Observer* carried a report saying that the poor quality of blooms that year at the Tower Hamlets Chrysanthemum Show was 'to be accounted for by the fact that many of our floricultural friends have been deprived of the "bits of ground" in which they took so much delight by the ruthless rage for buildings'.[19]

The Tower Hamlets Floricultural Society was started in 1859, mainly due to the enormous popularity of the chrysanthemum, which was 'the only flower the working man could successfully cultivate without an expense beyond his means,' according to Samuel Broome, who was head gardener of the Inner Temple and a keen chrysanthemum grower himself.[20] By the end of the nineteenth century, it was still possible to write that 'hundreds of amateurs grow collections where you would not think there was room to hang a clothes line.'[21]

Unlike the florists' shows of the eighteenth century where exhibitors met in inns and coffee houses and were exclusively all-male affairs, the East End Society shows positively encouraged female visitors while retaining all-male judging. Shows ran over two or three days attracting sometimes 'upwards of three thousand persons', and one held a concert one evening and a ball the next. Local nurserymen were able to compete in special categories, showing the ubiquitous pelargoniums, fuchsias and ferns, though the most of the entrants were amateurs such as Mr Groves, a postman, who entered plants in pots, a lot of cut flowers and a 'fine brace of cucumbers'.[22]

By the end of the nineteenth century, there was concern about the educational standards and recreational opportunities in the East End of London. The People's Palace in Mile End Road, opened by Queen Victoria in 1887, was seen as a suitable venue for a local horticultural society and competition open only to residents of Tower Hamlets and Hackney. Supported by the well-to-do including the queen herself, the Duke of Norfolk, the Duchess of Westminster and Lord Rothschild, the show had nine classes, including ones for 'plants, window boxes, fern cases [and] cut flowers'.

The winner of the 'best in show' was a fuchsia bush measuring 4 feet by 3 feet and grown by a labourer, George Haydon, in the one room that he shared with his wife near Mile End Road. Plant growing had come a long way since James Lee had found that first fuchsia on the sailor's widow's windowsill over 100 years before. Although the lower classes may not have had access to Wardian cases or been able to read Shirley Hibberd's *Rustic Adornments for Homes of Taste*, it would be wrong to assume that plants were not important to them. Certain plants became symbols of much soughtt-after respectability, as C. H. Rolph recalls in his memoirs of growing up in a poor working-class home in Finsbury Park in 1906.

I think [our front parlour's] furnishing began eventually with the acquisition, in exchange for a vast collection of trading stamps, of a jardinière, in which was placed a big flower-pot containing – of course – an aspidistra. After that the curtains were slightly parted in the daytime so that passers-by could just see that we too had an aspidistra, but not the emptiness beyond.[23]

CHAPTER 12

FLOWER DECORATIONS

In early April 1912 there was great excitement in the nursery belonging to the Rochford family in Turnford in Hertfordshire. A new strain of *Araucaria excelsa*, the Norfolk Island pine, was brought to the nursery. The new sport had fronds that were edged with silver and it was decided to call it 'Silver Star' and show it later that year at the Shrewsbury Flower Show.

Business was good. Three years before, twenty-eight new glasshouses had been built and, two years later, it was decided to add more to the ever-growing Rochford acreage just north of London. Exports were up as well, especially to the United States. Staff were busy packing up an order for one of their best American customers, H. A. Dreer of Philadelphia. It comprised £1,000 worth of palms that were carefully placed inside their packing cases, 12 feet (3.5 m) long and 4feet (1.25 m) wide. They were then surrounded by protective straw, before being sent off to the docks for loading. Long-term Rochford's employee Charles Prior had spent three weeks sponging the palms so that they would arrive in pristine condition. They never got there; the ship transporting this precious order was the *Titanic*.

It would be superstitious to believe that this was an omen, though many people have seen the sinking of the *Titanic* as just that, but things were certainly going to change with regard to plants in the home in the new century – and Rochford's nursery lived through many of its ups and downs. In the short term, this was not a disaster for the nursery. Dreer's not only paid for the sunken palms but also immediately reordered and paid for replacements. *Araucaria* 'Silver Star' was an instant hit at the Shrewsbury show and sold for the high price of one guinea, though it later disappeared from Rochford's lists completely during the First World War never to return.

Despite of the expansion of Rochford's nursery in the early years of the twentieth century, there was no doubt that people's tastes in plants were changing, just as they were in home decoration and garden design. In 1883, William Robinson, who was so dismissive of the English conservatory, had published his seminal work, *The English Flower Garden*. By 1903, it was on its eighth edition and sixth reprint, and had instigated a move in gardening style away from the fussy and formal bedding of the high Victorian era to a more naturalist look. New houses rarely had conservatories attached since they seemed to symbolize the barrier between the interior and the garden. Even plant hunting seemed to move from the tropical rainforests to chilly mountainsides, and many plants that were previously overcosseted in hot-houses such as camellias were found to be hardier than first thought.

The influence of William Morris on interior design was still strong. But by 1900, architect C. F. A. Voysey (1857–1941) was designing homes that were light with all white walls and even panelling. It was, said a colleague, 'as if Spring had come all of a sudden'.[1] Since the Arts and Crafts Exhibition of 1888, there was a shift towards the idealization of a natural, country or cottage garden style. Domestically, interest in the vernacular increased with the designs of architect Edwin Lutyens (1869–1944). But it was the partnership between Lutyens and Gertrude Jekyll, who had written the chapter on colour in Robinson's *English Flower Garden*, which was to have the most lasting effect on flowers and plants in the home in the early twentieth century.

Gertrude Jekyll (1843–1932) is known as one of the greatest influences on gardening style in the Edwardian period. Along with William Robinson, Jekyll banished stylized bedding from English gardens and stimulated thoughtful planting with colour schemes worthy of a painter's palette. She had been an artist until her sight began to fail. Yet it was her later writings that were so influential. One of Gertrude Jekyll's smaller and less well-known books is *Flower Decoration in the House* published in 1907. She was one of the first post-Victorians to promote the use in the house of cut flowers and shrubs from the garden.

Jekyll held strong opinions and was no less strident on the topic of what she called 'room-plants'. She would only countenance palms in large conservatories but rarely in living rooms: 'How often does one see in London, in quite a small room, quite a large Palm, with perhaps three leaves on long, naked stems; a thing utterly absurd in proportion.' She forgave the use of aspidistras because they 'always look well [and] are the most long-suffering of plants'.[2]

Jekyll despaired of the lack of well-designed containers available. 'Quantities of things are in the market, but with few exceptions, the quality of the design is not such as to make them acceptable in the best class of room.'[3] Jekyll had strong opinions not only on suitable containers but also on what they should be called. One gets a sense of how important even this apparently abstract problem was to her as part of the complete picture in the way that she mused over this terminology.

There are some English words which have no equivalent in French, but then there a great many more French words . . . for which we have no English. One of these is *jardinière*. Even in French it does not quite rightly express its meaning, because the obvious meaning of *jardinière*, is female gardener, whereas what we understand by it . . . is a receptacle for holding pot-plants. 'Receptacle' is quite a good word but has a certain stiffness. One writes 'receptacle,' but one scarcely says it. 'Pot-holder' is uncouth – loutish. 'Receiver" sounds like part of a lamp. 'Holder' is perhaps a little less rude than 'pot-holder,' and yet has some displeasing, though, perhaps, intangible taint . . . For flimsier things that veil the homely garden-pot we have also no word, whereas the French have *cache-pot*. But this sounds like a soldier's rifle, and is still more undesirable for acclimatisation. I therefore beg leave to say 'holder' until some better word may come, rejecting *jardinière* as both exotic and cumbersome.[4]

One wonders what Miss Jekyll would have thought of the pretensions of late twentieth-century indoor gardeners who happily used both *cache-pot* and the exotic and cumbersome *jardinière*. She was, in fact, a great fan of the French and thought that they were particularly careful and successful in setting up groups of pot plants.

They will put together one or two Crotons or Caladiums with Ferns, the whole surmounted by the feathery sprays of a beautifully grown young Cocos Palm. The kinds of foliage are sufficiently diversified to show off the several forms of beautiful plant-life in the best kind of contrast – the kind that is in fact a perfect harmony.[5]

Ferns and palms were acceptable to Jekyll if they were well chosen. But she also urged her readers to be more adventurous in their choice of 'room-plants', especially those that could be forced into early flowering: *Staphylea colchica* (Colchis bladdernut) and *Olearia phlogopappa* (dusty daisy bush) as opposed to 'such hackneyed things as *Spiraea japonica* and berried Solanum'.[6] *Begonia metallica, Hosta grandiflora* and the common polypody fern (*Polypodium vulgare*) were also recommended.

Among those taken up with the new style of natural gardening enough to write about it was Maria Theresa Earle. Mrs Earle, an upper-middle-class housewife, lived in a house in Bryanston Square in London during the winter, and in Cobham, Surrey, in the summer, where she gardened on what she called 'a small piece of flat ground surrounding an ordinary suburban house. Kitchen-garden, flower-garden, house and drive can scarcely cover more than two acres.'[7]

A keen plantswoman, Mrs Earle not only wrote about her Surrey garden but also described the plants she kept in her London drawing room to cheer her through the winter months. It is a revealing list: pots of common ivy on the side ledge of the large windows; repeating Miss Jekyll's phrase, two 'long-suffering' aspidistras, one plain, one variegated; and two sorts of India-rubber plants, *Ficus elastica* and *f. elastica indica*. On the windowsill is an *Anthericum liliago variegatum* (St Bernard's lily) while in the middle of the room is a Victorian favourite, *Pandanus veitchii*. This, she said – like most of us – 'does not mind the heat of the fire, but resents frost on the window-pane'.[8]

Her collection of cut flowers is impressive: *Chorizema cordata* (the Australian flame pea), 'sweet-smelling Geranium leaves', *Chimonanthus fragrans*, Neapolitan violets, hyacinths, branches of *Physalis alkekengi* (winter cherry), the double plum *(Prunus spinosa 'Flore Plena')*, and, for foliage, *Magnolia grandiflora*. Completing the display are two 'bright-green olive jars that came from Spain, into which are stuck large bunches of the white seed-vessels of Honesty and some flowers of Everlastings (*Helichrysum bracteatum*)'.[9]

No mention of ferns or Wardian cases, no elaborate displays of tropical hot-house plants, even palms do not appear in Mrs Earle's 'dark London room'. Instead, stems of shrubs from her country garden were displayed in Indian and Japanese vases reflecting the passion for Oriental designs that was sweeping across middle-class drawing rooms at the end of the nineteenth century. Even among the upper middle classes who still had the staff to look after exotics, there was a move away from the excesses of the high Victorian age towards a more naturalist look as reflected in the writing of Robinson and Jekyll and the architecture of Lutyens.

It was no longer fashionable to stuff a room with palms and ferns just as it was no longer fashionable to cover surfaces with heavy velvet drapery dotted with dust-gathering ornaments. Rooms were made lighter with white-painted panelling. Even the ordinary terraced house became more uncluttered as light oak furniture replaced the ornate mahogany of the previous century.

Domestic life was beginning to change with the arrival of underground trains allowing the middle class to chase the suburban life even further away from the fumes of the centre of London. The 'jerry-built' terraced developments of the nineteenth century were criticized as the ideals of 'garden cities' took hold. The architects of developments such as Letchworth and Hampstead Garden Suburb attempted to bring a new standard of living to suburban housing, with picket fences, communal greens spaces, and a 'cottagey' feel to the houses in keeping with the 'back to nature' movement that was so popular. These houses did not have conservatories or even greenhouses. Naturalist planting of herbaceous plants was encouraged; this was no longer the place for exotics and elaborate bedding.

Daily life was to change even more with the start of the First World War. For the first couple of years, the war did not seem to make that much difference to the trade in hot-house plants. Rochford's had to start employing women in their propagating houses as their male staff were called up. They were still able to supply a wide variety of plants in 1915, from pot roses, begonias, lilies of the valley and hydrangeas to the old favourites: dracaenas, crotons, aspidistras, aralias and araucarias. Vast varieties of poinsettias (*Euphorbia pulcherrima*) over two metres tall were available for Christmas. However, this did not last and soon the importing restrictions meant that it was impossible to buy replacement stock from abroad. Vegetables were more important than decorative plants and flowers and no one had the staff to look after luxurious hothouses any more. In 1920, the Great Conservatory built by Joseph Paxton at Chatsworth to house the exotic plant collection of the 6th Duke of Devonshire was blown up on the orders of the 9th Duke. Such extravagance seemed out of step with the time.

In more modest homes, it was also the end of one era of plants and the start of another. Modernism was creeping into domestic design, and the cactus was one of the few plants that looked as though it might belong in that sort of stern surrounding. Famous modernist buildings such as the Highpoint flats in North London included planting spaces in the lobby but these were filled with cacti and succulents. Even in traditional homes, clutter was cleared away as a neo-Georgian revival took hold. Between 1919 and 1939 nearly four million new homes were built across Britain, the majority going to middle-class house buyers.

The domestic routine was changing: 'the servant problem' meant that few homes had live-in help and houses were designed to cater for the wife doing the domestic work.

With space at a premium, the idea of the 'parlour', or one room that was kept for best, was falling out of favour. The garden was increasingly seen as a male preserve, a form of relaxation at the weekend when the husband was home from work, while the wife was expected to keep the home to a suitably high standard depending on their class position. Who can forget the humiliation of interwar writer E. M. Delafield's heroine in *The Diary of a Provincial Lady*, constantly agonizing over the indoor bulbs that will not come up while those of her wealthy neighbour Lady Boxe always bloomed on time? There was little time for labour-intensive conservatories, or the money to run them. In their place, however, there was a revival of a craft that had become an art form during the Victorian period: flower arranging.

As long as there were containers to put them in, flowers had been cut and brought into the home, as evidence from Egyptian and Roman remains confirm. During the Victorian period, flower arranging had reached heights (or lows depending on your taste) of contrivance and elaborate detailing. In upper-class homes, this was rarely the work of the mistress of the house. It fell to the gardener to produce endless complicated displays when the family was in residence, hence the publication of works such as that from the Duke of Grafton's head gardener, T. C. March, *Flower and Fruit Decoration*. Lower down the social scale, middle-class housewives tried to emulate such grandeur using designs found in *Floral Decorations for Dwelling Houses* by Annie Hassard.

Bouquets, nosegays and corsages were made professionally by the ever-growing number of professional florists such as Wills & Segar across the country. Floristry had become a popular path for young women who, whether by their own choice or not, wanted to get out of service. It was not something a middle-class girl would ever dream of doing as a career. There was also a snobbism attached to the arranging of flowers in the home. Since the start of the twentieth century when Victorian fussiness had fallen out of favour, it was considered poor taste to mix varieties of flowers in a vase since it might look as though you did not have a garden large enough to grow sufficient of one variety. So when a middle-class woman starting not just mixing flowers but including vegetables in her arrangements and then opened a shop to sell them, it was nothing short of revolutionary.

The woman was Constance Spry, whose name has become synonymous with the best of flower arranging, so it is hard for us to realize just how shocking her arrangements seemed when they first appeared in the late 1920s and early 1930s. Such was their success however, it enabled her to open a shop in Pimlico which she called 'Flower Decorations' to distinguish it from the professional floristry style she disapproved of. *Flower Decoration* was also the name of her first book, published in 1934. In it, she rarely mentions plants in pots, not surprising since her great loves were cut flowers and garden shrubs. When she does, she is surprisingly against one of the oldest forms of plant decoration in the home.

> One is sometimes asked to fill a fire-place with growing plants and ferns, or cut flowers and leaves. For a private house I am usually averse from this practice. The flowers look out of place, and the fire-place looks far better left in its normal state, especially if the grate is filled with the nicest logs that can be found. Silver-barked trees provide the best logs for this purpose.[10]

As the Second World War approached, the future looked bleak for plants in the home. While flower arranging was extremely popular, with clubs and competitions being run across the country, few homes had anything other than easiest of houseplants on display, the cactus and the rubber plant. These, said the *Architectural Review* in 1952, had become the clichés of the 1920s and 1930s as much as the aspidistra had of the Victorian era.

> The rise of the Cactus and its allied family occurred at the same time as a taste for the naiveté of the paintings of Le Douanier, and African sculpture, a pre-possession with pure form in architecture and a thorough going distaste of the exuberance in interior decoration of the Victorians and Edwardians.[11]

Although cactus plants were known in Britain for at least two centuries – Richard Bradley (1688–1732) had written his sumptuous *History of Succulent Plants* in 1716 – they had never fitted into the domestic scene before and were more likely to have been found in the specialist greenhouse or conservatory out of harm's way.

There is no doubt that while the British did not embrace modernism to the extent that they did on Continental Europe, anything vaguely Victorian was totally frowned upon as dated and vulgar. This change in taste combined with the devastating economic effects of the Second World War meant that businesses such as Rochford's nursery suffered enormously. When Thomas Rochford III returned from the war, it was to find a nursery in total disarray. With poor wartime management, greenhouses and boilers all needed repair, wartime controls were still in place, and staff were in short supply in spite of a handful of German prisoners-of-war drafted in.

Rochford decided to take a gamble and prune the pot plant list right back to only those that he calculated might be profitable: hydrangeas, Pteris ferns, cyclamen, crotons, heaths, geraniums and Kentia palms, for which he managed to obtain a licence to import 250,000 seeds. The nursery's stock of palms was cut to one-fifth its pre-war level and all other decorative plants were drastically reduced in number. The late 1940s was no time to take risks.

But sometimes fate takes a hand and paths cross. In 1947, Rochford's were approached by Constance Spry's business manager and asked to propagate nine new varieties of indoor ivies and a cissus grape ivy that Mrs Spry had just brought back from America. She was keen to introduce more unusual plants and leaf textures into her shop, by now in Mayfair, to sell alongside her flower arrangements. Such was the influence of Constance Spry, if Rochford's were successful, it would mean not just the saving of the nursery but a new wave of interest in plants for the home. Tom Rochford did not hesitate for a moment.

CHAPTER 13

'NO HOME IS COMPLETE WITHOUT LIVING PLANTS'

On 3 May 1951 King George V opened the Festival of Britain exhibition on the South Bank of London's Thames. Designed to lift the spirits of a war-weary nation, much of the focus of the exhibits was to show how a modern Britain was emerging through architecture and design. Modern ideas were taking hold not just for house design but for furniture as well. Scandinavian style seemed fresh and clean and unlike anything seen in Britain before. Their use of plants in the home was far removed from the cliché of the 1930s cactus and rubber plant. This was picked up by the interior designers of the time and, declared the *Architectural Review* in 1952, 'now in the fifties of this century, there are signs of a revival of the taste for room plants.'[1]

When six years later Prime Minister Harold Macmillan told post-war Britain that 'most of our people have never had it so good', it did seem that all the deprivations of the war years were over. Unemployment and inflation were low, rationing and shortages a thing of the past. More families were able to own their own homes and Britain was rebuilt not just to cope with an increasing population but also to deliver what seemed at the time to be more practical housing solutions.

In 1951 few households had live-in servants. Women who had acquired a degree of emancipation during the Second World War found themselves back in the kitchen once the preserve of domestic help. New labour-saving equipment such as washing machines and vacuum cleaners became more affordable. High-rise blocks of flats replaced antiquated housing stock across the country and central heating in its various forms gradually replaced the open fires that were time-consuming and filthy. The Clean Air Act of 1956 began the radical change that saw the gradual disappearance of city smogs and the arrival of cleaner homes. There was still concern about the effects of gas fumes on plants until the arrival of natural gas from the North Sea in the 1970s.

For many families the price for all this modernization was the loss of what little green space they may have had. Life became more home-centred but, more often than not, home was now a flat with barely a balcony. Magazines such as *Ideal Home* and *Good Housekeeping* focused on making these new homes the perfect place for the work-weary husband to come back to. In the suburbs, wives with frilly pinafores spent their days becoming 'domestic goddesses', cooking recipes from *Woman's Own* and trying to create homes that were never going to be as spacious as the ones they saw on the American situation comedies filling the television screens of Britain.

In the low-inflation, home-centred society that was post-war Britain, it is not surprising that houseplants had a new surge of popularity. Thanks to the likes of enterprising nurseryman Thomas Rochford, they were a relatively cheap way of introducing greenery into smaller houses and flats. They also seemed to bring a touch of modernity as well. Social commentator Osbert Lancaster wrote in 1959, 'architect[s] . . . vigorously encouraged the cultivation of ivy, philodendra and other climbing plants upstairs, downstairs and in my lady's parlour.'[2]

Although the majority of plants grown by nurseries such as Rochford's had been available for nearly 100 years, since their popularity waned between the wars, some had rarely been seen and were 'rediscovered'. Having a foliage-laden home may have fallen out of fashion at the start of the twentieth century, but in the second half of the century, it suddenly appeared the latest way of decorating your home. In the words of Michael Flanders and Donald Swann in 1956, in their revue 'Design for Living'.

The garden's full of furniture
And the house is full of plants!
Oh, it doesn't make for comfort
But it simply has to be
'Cos we're ever so terribly up-to-date,
comptemporary-ry!
. . . ivy everywhere!
You musn't be surprised to meet a cactus on the stair
But we call it home sweet home.[3]

Public spaces that had long banished the dusty palm also rediscovered pot plants for indoor decoration. Plantsman Roy Lancaster, then a young trainee gardener with the Bolton Parks Department in the 1950s, remembers the wide range of indoor plants specifically grown for social functions, in particular the annual Mayor's Ball.

Splendid displays of exotic plants were arranged and staged in the Albert Hall in Bolton's civic centre. Crotons, coleus, streptocarpus, achimenes, gloxinias and much else were used in good numbers to stun and delight the guests as they attended. It was an event repeated in civic halls countrywide and highlighted the glory years of corporation parks departments whose glasshouses were like mini crystal palaces ruled by stern foremen skilled in the arts of quality cultivation.[4]

In the late 1940s, Thomas Rochford had struggled to get supplies of plants to rebuild stocks at his nursery. He had obtained propagating material of aralias and monsteras from Scandinavia. He bought azaleas and *Ficus elastica*, which quickly became a best-seller, from Belgium. By the end of 1951, the Festival of Britain year, *Country Life* reported that it 'was the first year nurserymen remember when the sale of pot plants both green and flowering never ceased'.[5]

The following year Tom Rochford started using the term 'houseplants' to cover all the pot plants, both flowering and 'foliage', that the nursery grew and would become famous for. Initially, nurserymen at Covent Garden Market did not share his belief, worried that the lasting qualities of these plants would lose them profit in contrast to cut flowers, and calling them 'Rochford's Folly'. They were wrong: the aim was to grow 250,000 'houseplants'. By the mid-1950s Rochford's were growing more than a million plants from 117 different varieties.

One of the most popular was *Ficus elastica* 'Decora', an improved version of *F. elastica*. Its regained popularity was perhaps to do with its modern 'statement' look but probably more to do with its easy-care regime. The nursery produced 100,000 plants a year, many of which were transported across the country in Rochford's familiar green vans decorated on the side with a picture of a large *F. e. decora*, complete with the slogan, 'No home is complete without living plants.'

Rochford's slogan epitomized the change in attitude to indoor plants in the post-war years. One plant in particular became a passion among home growers. In the early 1950s, there were two small horticultural societies, one of which specialized in houseplants and another devoted to encouraging the growing of saintpaulias, the African violet. It was soon realized that most of the members belonged to both societies so in 1956 they merged. Such was the passion for growing saintpaulias that that name took precedence and the new group became the Saintpaulia & Houseplant Society, the name it keeps to this day.

The African violet may be one of the newest introductions of plants into the home but its success was not surprising. It does not require the special conditions that orchids demand, is not difficult to propagate, and cared for correctly can be in flower for many months of the year.

It has not always been so. In 1892 Baron von St Paul-Illaire was the governor of an area which included the Usambara Mountains in remote northern Tanzania. In his spare time, he combed the countryside for new plants and made the first discovery of a small plant with bluish-purple flowers. This he sent to his father, who in turn passed it on to his friend Hermann Wendland, director of Berlin's Royal Botanic Garden, who named it after the baron's family, *Saintpaulia ionantha*.

The original species was difficult to grow but seed was disributed in Germany and Britain together with another Tanzanian discovery, *S. confusa*. When seed arrived in America in 1925, Armacost & Royston, a Los Angeles based nursery, recognized its potential as a houseplant. Their first introduction, 'Blue Boy', went on sale in 1927. Most of the interest was in America and cross-breeding in 1939 produced double blue flowers. In 1940 a single pink seedling was named 'Pink Beauty' and in 1941 the first variegated leaf variety appeared.

Post-war Britain became gripped by saintpaulia fever and the 1960s saw the introduction of star-shaped flowers and fancy-edged petals. Throughout the 1960s and 1970s, Rochford's were famous for their saintpaulias and it seemed that no flower basket was complete without one. There are now over 2,000 varieties with seven different leaf shapes ranging from 'boy' (standard plain green leaf) to 'spoon', which has rolled-up edges, and eight different flower categories with clear distinctions between ruffled and fringed. There is even a miniature variety that can be grown in a wine glass, the ultimate indoor plant. Perhaps that is why a strain developed in the early 1970s by Rochford's, called 'Endurance', designed to be frost-hardy and named after Antarctic adventurers, was never a success. For the African violet is the quintessential houseplant and more than any other would look wrong in the garden when its place has always been on the windowsill.

In the 1950s information on houseplants was still relatively hard to find. Richard Gilbert, for many years president of the Saintpaulia & Houseplant Society, remembers returning from the war to help in his mother's market garden business. In 1950 he bought a copy of American writer Montague Free's book, *All About House Plants*.

North America was well ahead of Europe at this stage, especially in terms of what they could grow, recalls Gilbert. 'The USA with steam heating and a wide temperature range through its many states found climbing aroids such as philodendron, scindapsis and syngium thrived and low-growing creepers from the forest floor of tropical and sub-tropical countries did well with warm and filtered light.'[6] Bringing back a small potted bougainvillea from Denmark, 'a plant I had not seen before (nor had the Customs official)', was the start of a life-long love of houseplants for Gilbert. Denmark was by now established as one of the centres of European houseplant production. As Osbert Lancaster noted, 'The Cacti of the Middle European 'thirties were now outclassed by extraordinary growths, conceived on the Amazon and nurtured in the hothouses of Copenhagen.'[7]

It was around this time that the BBC first starting broadcasting a monthly gardening programme called 'Gardening Club' which introduced Percy Thrower, who was to become the first television gardening celebrity. The programme was enormously popular in spite of being studio-based with microphones concealed in pots of soil. Tom Rochford was one of Thrower's first guests giving advice on all sorts of houseplant problems. The response was phenomenal with the nursery receiving over 2,500 letters, which all had to be answered individually. This led to the establishment of a nursery advisory service; purchasers were given leaflets and pamphlets and florists were supplied with 'Rochford folders' with plant suggestions.

In the early 1960s, the plant labels were also redesigned to include information on care, position and temperature. They were colour-coded, pink for *Easy*, blue for *Intermediate*, and yellow for *Delicate*. We take for granted having such information on supermarket buys, but before Rochford's highly recognizable labels were introduced there was little in the way of help for the amateur houseplant gardener from the nurseries themselves.

Although the Architectural Press had published Margaret E. Jones and H. F. Clark's small but influential book, *Indoor Plants and Gardens,* in 1952, publishers, on the whole, were slow to capitalize on the growing interest in plants in the home. It may have been with some reluctance then that Pan Britannica Ltd, the fertilizer manufacturer, agreed to publish a booklet on houseplants in 1960, suggested by one of their employees, David Hessayon, as a follow up to his first booklet on gardening.

As with Rochford and his labelling system, Hessayon was someone else who believed that spelling things out in a simple, clear style was the best way to help people get the most from their plants. The booklet was *Be Your Own House Plant Expert*. It has gone down not just in gardening history, but also in publishing history. The book has sold fourteen million copies and is claimed to be the biggest-selling reference book of all time after the Bible. Imitators have slowly followed but few have come close to the successful formula that Hessayon has stuck to for over sixty years throughout his 'Expert' range of books. It is estimated that one in two households in Britain have at least one of his gardening books on their shelves – but it was the book on houseplants that was the most successful and helped Pan Britannica's product, Baby Bio, to become synonymous with houseplant food.

With magazines and newspapers as diverse as *Amateur Gardening, Housewife* and the *Daily Telegraph* now devoting many column inches to houseplants, their popularity was assured. But there were essential differences in the use of plants in the 1950s and 1960s to the way they had been used in nineteenth-century homes. Gone were the labour-intensive conservatories, damp ferneries, ornate jardinières and elaborate Wardian cases. In their place came angular plant stands, bamboo trellis supports and macramé hanging basket holders. For the first time in over half a century, plants were once more seen as important features of domestic design and worthy of interior designers' interest. This was in no small part due to the influence of the Scandinavians. 'Curious wooden grilles appeared, inexplicably jutting out at right angles into the logical living-rooms of Gothenburg and New Canaan, up which ivy and philodendron were lovingly trained,' wrote Osbert Lancaster in his 1959 satirical history of architecture.[8] Jones and Clark's 1952 book featured plant displays in Arne Jacobsen's house in Denmark. In Britain, young designers at the Royal College of Art were encouraged to produce useable plant boxes and trays. These were featured in the book as well as a metal plant stand designed specifically for the Architectural Press by a young man named Terence Conran.

The much-maligned macramé hanging plant holder did not spring from the RCA but from the craze for crafts in the 1960s and 1970s. By this stage, the market was flooded with 'how-to' books on houseplants, all no doubt hoping to emulate Dr Hessayon's success. Few did, though the continuing coverage, especially in women's magazines, continued to fuel an enthusiasm particularly for foliage plants such as the spider plant (*Chlorophytum comosum*), which seemed to fit in particularly well with the interior design tastes of the period.

In 1969 *Woman's Own* was one of several magazines to publish their own guide to indoor plants, written by William Davidson. Although this was a serious book on plant care, it did contain some rather eccentric advice – or perhaps it just sheds a little light on what really did go on in the Swinging Sixties!

> Parties and House Plants Don't Agree . . . at party time plants will be much safer if they are transferred to an upstairs bedroom. Guests who are having just one more drink pressed on them are not above emptying the unwanted alcohol into the convenient receptacle provided by a plant pot! The damage does not become apparent until some time later, and the plant's sudden failure usually remains a mystery.[9]

Watering, wrote Davidson, was key and 'the failure of almost 75 per cent of all the plants that eventually find their way to the dustbin can be traced to the over-indulgent housewife who is ever ready with the watering can.' However, even he thought that the old nurseryman's trick of tapping pots with a cotton reel fixed to the end of a long cane to test whether the pot had dried out was a little too scientific for his readers. 'The mind boggles at the thought of the average owner of a few indoor plants performing this percussion exercise, and trying to decide whether it should be one or two egg-cupfuls of water.'[10]

Changes were happening in the industry that would make such a test impossible. Plastic pots replaced the old terracotta pots for many houseplants. Although terracotta's water-holding capacity was lost, plastic was cheaper, lighter and less liable to damage. It was also more hygienic – and more disposable. The plant trade was modernizing but even in the early 1970s many homes still had gas fires and fumes remained a problem, as Davidson acknowledged. Central heating was a luxury for many people and, even with it installed, homes were often kept at a lower temperature than the ubiquitous 21°C we are used to throughout our homes.

In the relatively small world of houseplant experts, it does not come as a surprise to find that *Woman's Own*'s author was none other than Rochford's Show Manager, William 'Jock' Davidson. Davidson wrote over half a dozen such books during the 1960s and 1970s. Rochford's had begun exhibiting at the Royal Horticultural Society's regular shows in the early 1950s and won successive awards for their outstanding contributions to houseplant varieties in Britain. Betty Rochford, Tom's wife, had been in charge of designing their displays since 1959, where her talent at plant arranging led the firm to be chosen to represent the British Plant and Greenhouse group at the prestigious Paris *Floralies* trade exhibition. Out went the serried rows of pots on trestle tables and in came staged displays of plants with a tropical lush look that we take for granted now at shows such as Chelsea.

By 1970, Rochford's were growing around 400 different varieties and species of foliage and flowering houseplants. Plants were now grown not only in homes but in offices, hotels and banks as well. This prompted a new wave of businesses catering for the maintenance of these plants, echoing the contract rental businesses of the nineteenth century such as James Cochran and Mr Mangles. Unable to rely on regular watering, many of these firms installed hydroponic units where the plants were grown without soil supported in an inert medium such as Leca and fed through water.

Although bulbs had been grown for three centuries in water, it was not until the 1930s that American scientists developed the idea of growing a variety of plants purely in water. By the Second World War, this was used as a suggested method to provide troops with fresh vegetables whatever the soil. Houseplant growers had to wait until the 1960s for it to become commercially available. Although there was a spate of 'self-watering' pots available in the 1970s and 1980s, they never caught on in the home as they did in the office environment. As an 'easy-care' option, hydroponics are only really suitable for large plants and since the containers themselves are rarely cheap, homeowners preferred to stay with the wide range of plastic pots and cachepots available.

In spite of the advanced tissue culture propagation techniques available, British suppliers of houseplants relied more and more on imported plants from Holland, Italy and lately the Far East. In the early 1970s, Rochford's began to cut back on the number of green or foliage houseplants they grew and moved more into the flowering pot plant market. The nursery was famous for its prize-winning saintpaulias but it also produced millions of poinsettias, azaleas and Christmas cactuses. However, increasingly Denmark, Holland and Belgium were producing houseplants in such enormous numbers that it no longer became economically viable for the few British producers to carry on. By the 1980s, the nursery finally closed, the last major British houseplant nursery, to make way for foreign importers, leaving only a handful of specialist nurseries such as Dibleys and Fibrex, holders of national collections of streptocarpus, and pelargoniums and hedera, respectively.

By the end of the twentieth century, houseplants were falling out of favour once again. Market research done by the Flowers and Plants Association in the late 1990s showed that while older people were willing to give houseplants the care and attention they needed, the younger attitude, particularly among women, was that they were just an extra burden, yet one more thing to look after once work was finished, the house cleaned, the dog fed and children put to bed. Time had become a precious commodity and houseplants just were not 'instant' enough for the next generation.

CHAPTER 14

'GOOD FOR YOUR HEALTH AND GOOD FOR YOUR SOUL'

In 2001, prize-winning garden designer Andy Sturgeon proclaimed that houseplants are 'good news'. 'They're good for your health and good for your soul. They can be cool, stylish, sexy even, but they should be part of your room design not some apologetic afterthought.'[1] With sections in his book on 'kitsch' plants including *Maranta leuconeura, Calathea crocata,* cockscomb (*Celosia*) and *Anthurium scherzerianum* (cock-on-a-plate) and 'pariahs' such as polka-dot plants (*Hypoestes phyllostachya*), African violets, rubber plants and Rex begonias, houseplants are once more must-have interior accessories.

Zamioculcas zamiifolia, a tongue-twister of a name, is typical of the newest introductions to popular houseplant lists. Zamioculcas originates from the tropical African areas of Tanzania and Zanzibar – seemingly so new that it appears in few houseplant care books. Since Dutch nurseries started wide-scale commercial propagation of zamioculcas around 1996, it has become a design favourite because of its strong lines and easy-care regime. Yet this is no Johnny-come-lately. There was an illustration of the species type of zamioculcas in Loddiges's *Botanical Cabinet* in 1828. *Z. zamiifolia* was discovered in the late nineteenth century but not introduced until the end of the twentieth.

While the days of plant hunters bringing back thousands of new varieties were over by the beginning of the twentieth century, discoveries were still made that had far-reaching influences over the houseplant market. In the early 1900s *Schlumbergera*, or the Christmas cactus, was introduced, named after Frederick Schlumberg. New varieties of citrus still arrived in the West. *Citrus* 'Meyer's Lemon' was introduced to the United States from China in 1908, while the smaller Calamondin orange, *Citrus mitis,* was a much later arrival, perfect for windowsill growing where it soon became laden with small fruits.

The enormously popular x *Fatshedera lizei* was the result of cross-breeding by the Lizé Frères nursery of Nantes in 1912. Its parents were *Fatsia japonica* 'Moseri' and the Irish ivy, *Hedera hibernica*. In 1952, Norfolk-born plant collector L. Maurice Mason brought the iron-cross begonia, *B. masoniana*, back from Singapore, since when it has become one of the most popular of the several thousand begonia species and hybrids.

Requiring similar conditions to begonias, gesneriads have produced many new exciting introductions for keen houseplant growers. In addition to saintpaulias, streptocarpus were first introduced into Europe in the early 1800s. *S. rexii* was flowering at Kew in 1827, after which hybridization began in earnest. The introduction of *S.* 'Constant Nymph' in 1947 by W. J. C. Laurence at the John Innes Institute, began the species's popularity as a flowering pot plant. Other gesneriads such as achimenes, the hot water plant, and columnea, the goldfish plant, are also popular among enthusiasts.

With the exception of fatshedera, all these houseplants involve some care to produce regular flowering. In contrast, *Z. zamiifolia* is a slow-growing stately foliage plant, making it relatively expensive to buy but highly desirable. With firm succulent-like leaves, it is happy with relatively low light levels and is trouble-free. With such characteristics, zamioculcas has many similar features to other easy-care plants such as the Victorian favourite, the aspidistra, and mother-in-law's tongue, *Sansevieria trifasciata*. Only time will tell whether it will have similar scorn poured on it later in the twenty-first century.

Just as interior design never stays still, so fashions in houseplants always seem to be on the move. In today's disposable society, houseplants, especially flowering plants, are seen as items to be thrown away as soon as they have faded. When you can buy an orchid for little more than the price of a bouquet of flowers, where is the incentive to keep it gathering dust on a back windowsill in the hope that it will flower again next year?

In 2004, the top four foliage and flowering plants sold in the United Kingdom were poinsettias, chrysanthemums, cyclamen and begonias. The same four plants were in the top four in 2000. Yet when asked what is their favourite houseplant, the public's taste is different. Here orchids top the list. This is not surprising given that they are much more widely available at more reasonable prices due to micro-propagation. Coming a close second is the peace lily, *Spathiphyllum wallisii*, due in no small part to its reputation as an eco-friendly houseplant and mopper-upper of air pollutants such as acetone, trichloroethylene, benzene and formaldehyde.

Forty years ago, research at NASA began to test the theory that houseplants could be used to clean the air of toxic chemicals from furnishings, household cleaners and building materials that build up in confined spaces. The results proved that houseplants should be not only an aesthetic feature of every home but also a way to improve indoor air quality. This is particularly important in offices with air conditioning. 'Sick building syndrome' can be reduced by low-emission materials and preventative maintenance. In homes, too, central heating and double glazing lead to poor air circulation. Foliage plants can 'clean' the air around and are, as Andy Sturgeon says, 'good for your health'.

Dr B. C. Wolverton, who worked on the NASA research, has come up with a list of fifty plants that can purify the air of both homes and offices. Among them were some old favourites that were at home in many Victorian parlours. Leading the battle against formaldehyde fumes is the Boston fern (*Nephrolepis exaltata* 'Bostoniensis'). Close behind it is the Victorian favourite, the rubber plant (*Ficus robusta* syn. *elastica*), the best of all the ficus family for removing chemical toxins from the air. A six-foot areca palm (*Chrysalidocarpus lutescens*) can transpire a litre of water into the air around it every twenty-four hours. It is also one of the most highly rated plants for removing indoor air toxins. The ubiquitous spider plant (*Chlorophytum comosum*) was one of the first plants NASA proved to be beneficial by removing pollutants.

Sturgeon's second point, that plants can be 'good for your soul', is a recent idea to the West but goes back centuries in the East. Feng Shui is used extensively in Eastern countries to improve the 'flow' of positive energy, or 'chi', through homes and offices and thereby bring health, wealth and good fortune to their inhabitants. If you have ever wondered why Chinese restaurants so regularly have a large money plant (*Crassula arborescens*) by their entrance, it is because it is traditionally seen as an auspicious plant, bringing increased prosperity to its owners.

Luckily the majority of plants suggested for either health or soul are easily available. But the many marvellous introductions of the last century are not so easy to come by. Figures from the Flower Council of Holland show that sales of houseplants have not changed much in the first decade of the twenty-first century. The tussle for a share of the houseplant market between the supermarkets and garden centres meant that most offered only a limited selection of plants. This was, and still is, especially so for supermarkets for whom cut flowers are more profitable than pot plants.

Within garden centres, according to one rueful British houseplant supplier, the biggest growth has been in coffee shops. Plantsman Roy Lancaster notes with regret that fine pot plants such as *Calomeria amaranthoides*, the incense plant, are now rarely grown except in botanic gardens and by a few specialists.[2] Retail outlets look for 'added value' in their houseplant sales, offering plants packed as ready-made gifts or with colour-coded containers making them appeal to people redecorating their homes rather than to keen gardeners. Sadly this also means that only the easy-care plants are widely sold, not just for the buyers' benefit but also for the benefit of the retailer who has to look after them until they are sold.

The boom in conservatory building that started in the 1970s sadly did not bring about a Victorian-style resurgence in the popularity of houseplants. Poor siting and ventilation meant that plants often struggled to survive in the blazing heat of the midday sun, while few were equipped with suitable drainage facilities to enable overhead watering for dampening down. While the side avenues of the Chelsea Flower Show may still be full of mock-Edwardian garden 'rooms', the majority will end up being more suitable for Queen Anne's evening supper parties than housing Mr Gosling's plant collections.

Fortunately, there will always be enthusiasts such as the stalwarts of Britain's Saintpaulia & Houseplant Society.[2] In the tradition of the florists of past centuries, they hold regular meetings at the Royal Horticultural Society's halls in central London, where leaf cuttings and stories are swapped. Their annual show demonstrates the high standards that can be achieved at home. While some plants are grown on windowsills, others are the product of hours of dedicated care and artificial light. But, according to the society's president, we are still years behind the American enthusiasts who go for high-tech darkened growing rooms and fully automated watering systems.

However limited the choice, pot plants are big business. In 2000, just one nursery in Amsterdam produced eighteen million orchids. Micro-propagation techniques using meristematic cells taken from bud and root tips make for near foolproof propagation. But customers want foolproof plants at home as well. If plants are to survive for more than just their flowering period, they must need minimal care conditions, which rule out so many interesting exotics and leave us with the usual suspects.

In the 400 years or so that we have brought plants into the home, there have been peaks and troughs of interest and enthusiasm. There have been surprises too: how skilled gardeners were in growing hardy perennial plants in pots to whip indoors when flowering was at its peak; the importance of scent, which allowed the most weedy looking plants such as mignonette to reign supreme for so long. Many plants that we associate with the high Victorian period had, in fact, been around for at least a century before, thanks to intrepid plant hunters worldwide. And improved technology in everything from water supplies to heat and light to transport had an impact on indoor plant growing for such a long period.

CONCLUSION

In November 2019, the quality British newspaper, *The Sunday Times*, made an astonishing claim. 'Plantfluencers [*sic*] [are] now paying more than £2,000 for the Chanel handbag of houseplants: *Monstera obliqua*.'[1] With no more details, it is hard to know the authenticity of this report. What is in no doubt is that the world of houseplants has changed dramatically since this book was first published in 2007. In just twelve years, houseplants have become status symbols across the world, reaching a new peak of popularity overshadowing that even of the nineteenth century. In 2019, the Royal Horticultural Society found that nearly three-quarters of adults had a houseplant in their home. Amazingly, the figure for sixteen- to twenty-four-year-olds was even higher. Eighty per cent owned an indoor plant.[2]

Houseplants are big business: in the UK alone, the indoor houseplant and flower market in 2018 was worth £2.2 billion.[3] While high figures for flowers might not be a surprise, it is the increase in houseplant sales that is causing a stir in the horticultural industry. An article in *The Garden*, the Royal Horticultural Society's journals in November 2019 reported figures from the Garden Centre Association showing indoor plants sales up 14 per cent in just two years.[4] However, the biggest increase came from the RHS's own garden centre at Wisley in Surrey where sales increased 62 per cent in one year. Little wonder the *Financial Times* and other broadsheet newspapers began to take an interest with articles such as 'Houseplants enjoy a growth spurt in popularity', 'Houseplants: The new bloom economy' and 'The one thing millennials haven't killed is houseplants'.[5]

This final chapter looks at how this 'green revolution' has come about in just over a decade. As mentioned at the beginning of this new edition, three major factors are involved: improved propagation techniques leading to increased availability and lower prices, changing lifestyles particularly of the millennial generation, and the phenomenal growth of social media.

Fashions in houseplants always been on the move. Their popularity has waxed and waned over the centuries. In today's disposable society, plants brought indoors, especially flowering plants, are often seen as disposable, to be thrown away as soon as they have faded. This is mainly because advances in micropropagation have led to dramatic price reductions. The almost ubiquitous moth orchid (phalaenopsis), for example, can now be bought for almost a quarter of what it would have cost twenty years ago.[6] There is little incentive to keep the orchid (not a particularly exciting foliage plant when not in flower) and get it to flower again the following year (easy as that is) when it costs less than a bunch of flowers to replace it with a new flowering specimen.

Other aspects of indoor horticultural technology have vastly improved in the last ten years. The market value of 'vertical farming', as it is known, has quadrupled in the US since 2013 to $2 billion, with predictions it will do so again by 2023 as the world looks for ways to produce healthy food without increased air miles.[7] Many see this as the future of vegetable farming as land space becomes increasingly at a premium the world over. The needs of these indoor farmers who grow salad greens and herbs without natural light have had a knock-on effect for the home grower. A quick trawl of the Internet brings up highly sophisticated 'natural light' indoor plant-growing systems aimed at the vast market for growing cannabis plants domestically, ostensibly for personal use. The benefit to the houseplant lover is that simple indoor lighting systems such as grow lights available from homes retailer IKEA allow homeowners to grow a much wider variety of plants without the worry of unstable indoor lighting conditions.

The majority of customers want fool-proof plants at home. If plants are to survive in the modern, centrally heated home, they must meet simple care conditions, which rule out many interesting exotics. While traditional garden centres have lagged behind in promoting indoor plant sales, the growth area has been in online sales. Specialist companies such as Hortology and Patch in the UK and The Sill in the US have done well tapping into this market. In 2018, The Sill sold over 100,000 plants to North American millennials. Patch had even greater success in the UK that year with 120,000 houseplants going into British homes.[8] Freddie Blackett started the business in 2015 aiming at young buyers with little or no experience of indoor gardening. All plants are marketed with reassuring friendly names such as 'Chaz the Swiss Cheese Plant' and 'Suzie the Snake Plant'. No botanical names to scare off the buyers, this is the top end of instant interior plant design with helpful simplified care instructions.

As we enter the 2020s, it is clear that one particular factor, unconnected with horticulture, has influenced indoor plant sales: lack of outdoor space for the millennial generation. Few are lucky enough to live in a property with a balcony let alone a garden. But the desire to bring a touch of the outdoors inside is strong. And one of the biggest drivers of the resurgence of interest in houseplants was the arrival of the social media website Pinterest in January 2010 followed in October that year by Instagram. As of May 2019, this photo-sharing website had 1 billion registered users.

It is not difficult to see why indoor plants have become phenomenally popular among a generation of millennials who regularly share images of their food and their pets. In the same vein, houseplants are easy to photograph with a mobile phone. As horticultural journalist and former gardening editor of *The Guardian*, Jane Perrone, points out, 'a variegated leaf looks good in a square more so than a border full of plants outside.'[9] A fanatical indoor plant collector herself since childhood, Perrone started a podcast, 'On the Ledge', in early 2017. Within three years, it has become one of the most popular UK podcasts in the 'home and garden' category, drawing in listeners from across the world, especially US listeners who are anxious to learn more about the plants in their care. Specialist topics range from terrariums – growing plants in glass containers, a revival from Victorian times though often sold with totally unsuitable succulents – to new crazes such as kokedama, the art of growing small plants in balls of moss, to aquascaping, a niche branch of aquarium-keeping that focuses on the artistic growing of underwater plants rather than the fish.

While there is an also ever-increasing number of houseplant fan pages on Facebook, it is Instagram that is awash with style 'influencers' such as Jamie Song and James Wong in the UK, Darryl Cheng in Canada, and Hilton Carter and Summer Rayne Oakes in the US, who have hundreds of thousands of followers. These are big names in the publishing industry as well and dozens of books, both practical and 'coffee table', are being published every year.

With this resurgence of interest in the care and display of indoor plants, in 2018 the RHS started a Houseplant and Cut Flower Advisory Group to include botanist, broadcaster, indoor plant fanatic and Instagram star, @botanygeek James Wong, and floral designer Jonathan Moseley.[10] In early 2020, the RHS also ran their first 'The Great Houseplant Takeover' at Wisley, a festival designed to draw in visitors during the long winter months. Other events took place at RHS Hyde Hall in Essex and Harlow Carr in North Yorkshire.

This has naturally helped increase sales of houseplants. With images of popular plants such as *Monstera deliciosa* (Swiss cheese plant), varieties of *Alocasia* (elephant's ears) and *Calathea* (prayer plant) constantly available on social media platforms from around the world, it is no surprise that the RHS found these varieties were their best-selling houseplants in 2019. Sales of *Alocasia*, particularly the dramatic *A. zebrina*, rocketed to ten times the previous year's figure while an astonishing 1,300+ *Calathea* also sold at their Wisley Plant Centre. None of these plants are new discoveries except to a new generation of plant owners who use large-leaved plants such as *Ficus lyrata*, the fiddle-leaf plant, to add statuesque greenery to their interiors. This plant in particular has become instantly recognizable from its frequent appearances in design magazines.

There has been one casualty: the Saintpaulia & Houseplant Society no longer exists, probably due to its ageing membership profile and lack of Internet presence. It also lost the enthusiasm of its president, Richard Gilbert, who died in 2009. That is not to say that plant societies that include plants grown indoors are disappearing. Both the British Streptocarpus Society and the British Cactus and Succulent Society are flourishing; the latter has over 100 regional groups. However, it is social media – Instagram, Facebook and Pinterest in particular – that have opened up world-wide opportunities for sharing knowledge that were inconceivable even fifteen years ago.

This passion for indoor plants has not been all good news. Some such as the variegated monstera are now so highly sought after that specialist nurseries are being targeted by 'handbag' thieves taking cuttings. While in the past this might have been seen as something of a grey area – gardeners are famously generous – it is one thing sharing a plant and quite another filling a backpack with valuable snippings. In December 2019, the Potted Elephant nursery in Portland, Oregon, was a victim to such a theft. The thief was apprehended and sentenced to a year on probation.[11] The restitution payment she also had to pay was of little comfort to owner Cory Jarrell since, in many cases, the mother plant had been damaged and was often irreplaceable. This is not unique to US nurseries. European botanical nurseries have also tragically been targeted given the unique nature of their collections.

With the increase in popularity of indoor plants, it is also not surprising that UK imports of live plants have jumped over 70per cent since 1999. Changes in the import laws to try and stop the spread of plant diseases may slow this down slightly, as might the aftermath of Brexit, but it is unlikely that British nurseries will ever become major suppliers again as they were in the early to mid-twentieth century, since they do not have the finances to do so and there are few government incentives. In contrast, Dutch growers do have such support and lead the way in terms of houseplant exports. While such imports are heavily regulated, according to UK government figures, there are now around 1,000 pests and diseases affecting trees and plants in the United Kingdom, many of which arrive in this country on imported plants.[12]

One of the horticultural industry's main selling points for houseplants in recent years has been their health benefits. With everyone becoming more aware of air pollution, various varieties of plants have increasingly been marketed for their abilities to mop these up. New research is now showing that it is not quite as simple as having a single peace lily in your kitchen. While researching for a PhD at the University of Birmingham, environmental consultant Curtis Gubb found that although plants can remove a variety of pollutants, a higher density is required than a few traditional potted plants can provide. His research now focuses on the benefits of 'green walls'. Even with such large coverage, there are many factors to be taken into consideration: 'correct environmental conditions . . . specific to each plant species and pollutant . . . the light levels, substrate moisture content and composition . . . alongside appropriate feeding and watering regimes to keep the plants functioning optimally'.[13]

The year 2020 has been designated the International Year of Plant Health with aims to help public awareness of plant hygiene. High on the list is the message of how dangerous it can be to bring cuttings back to the UK. The days of including cuttings in one's sponge bag must be over now that there is so much more awareness of the transmission of plant disease. But it is not only the keen horticultural holidaymaker who is to blame for importing potentially diseased plant material. There are also many unscrupulous professional plant hunters and sellers. While the movement of plants is increasingly being regulated, it is hard for buyers of houseplants in particular to know about their source. 'Houseplants are seen a commodity,' says herbalist and environmental campaigner Maya Thomas. She has concerns about sustainability. 'While this seems to be a boost for the economy . . . with notable benefits for mental health and well-being . . . we need to be thinking about the environmental impact of air/shipping miles and plastic packaging.'[14]

All this has not stopped the seemingly inexorable popularity of houseplants. In 2020, the RHS introduced a new competitive category for the world-famous Chelsea Flower Show (cancelled due to Covid-19) – 'Houseplant Studios'. Designers were encouraged to promote the benefits of indoor plants and provide inspiration for any room in the house, to show that no matter how much or little available natural light and regardless of size, everyone can enjoy growing plants indoors all the year round. Yet in October 2019, journalist and plant fanatic Alice Vincent posed the question: 'Are millennials at risk of killing the houseplant obsession they created?'[15] I think not – at least not yet. Fashions are notorious for going in cycles but, from past experience, this one has plenty of growth left in it.

PLANT LISTS

Plants introduced or discovered up to 1730

The lists are drawn from a variety of sources, some historical, some current. They do not aim to be definitive but are designed to give an indication of the variety of plants brought into the home at various times. It is always tricky to date plant introductions since there can be long gaps between a plant being discovered and its arrival in Britain. I have relied especially on the various works by the late John Harvey, *The World Atlas of House Plants* (ed. Anthony Huxley), Maggie Campbell-Culver's *The Origin of Plants* and others listed in the bibliography.

Starred plant names (*) are those recommended by Batty Langley for indoor display in *New Principles of Gardening* (1728).

Date	Botanical name	Historical name, Common name	Country or area of origin if known
Native	*Aquilegia vulgaris*	Columbine, granny's bonnet	
Native	*Buxus sempervirens*	Box tree, common box	
Native	*Leucanthemum vulgare*	Ox-eye daisy, Marguerite	
Native	*Narcissus pseudonarcissus*	Lent lily, wild daffodil	
Native	*Rosa rubiginosa**	Eglantine, sweet-briar	
Native	*Viola odorata**	Sweet violet	
Native	*Viola tricolor*	Heartsease, wild pansy	
*c.*900	*Lilium candidum**	White lily	
*c.*900	*Artemisia abrotanum*	Southernwood	
*c.*1260	*Matthiola incana**	Stock gillyflower, stock	S. Europe
*c.*1265	*Lavandula angustifolia*	Lavender spike, English lavender	W. Mediterranean
1275	*Erysimum cheiri**	Wallflower	S. Europe
*c.*1300	*Laurus nobilis*	Bay tree, sweet bay	Mediterranean
*c.*1300	*Lychnis chalcedonica**	Jerusalem cross, Maltese cross	
1338	*Rosmarinus officinalis*	Guard-robe, rosemary	Mediterranean
*c.*1340	*Ocimum basilicum**	Sweet basil, common basil	Asia
*c.*1350	*Crocus vernus**	Spanish saffron	Italy, Austria, E. Europe
1475	*Dianthus caryophyllus**	Carnation, gillyflower, clove-gillyflower	Spain
*c.*1500	*Jasminum officinale**	White jessamine, common jasmine	China
*c.*1540	*Antirrhinum majus*	Snapdragon	
1548	*Amaranthus tricolor*	Tricolor	
1548	*Capsicum annum**	Capiscum indicum, sweet pepper	N. America
1554	*Agave americana*	Century plant	C. America
1560	*Dianthus plumarius**	Sops in wine, pink	C. Europe
1560	*Viburnum tinus**	Laurus-tinus, Laurustinus	S. Europe
1562	*Myrtus communis*	Myrtle	Mediterranean
1568	*Mirabilis jalapa**	Marvel of Peru, Four o'clock flower	Mexico

Date	Botanical name	Historical name, Common name	Country or area of origin if known
1570	Celosia argentea var. cristata*	Coxcomb, prince's feather, Red fox, woolflower	Pan tropical
1570	Nigella damascena	Love-in-a-mist	Mediterranean
1573	Dianthus barbatus*	Sweet william	S. Europe
1577	Tulipa*	Tulip	Turkey
c.1580	Fritillaria imperialis*	Imperial, crown imperial	Turkey to Vienna, Iran to N. India
1585	Hylotelephium telephium (Sedum telephium)	Orpin[e], Witches' money-bags (US)	Mediterranean, Portugal
1595?	Citrus aurantium	Orange flowers, Seville orange, bitter orange	Tropical Asia
1596	Amaranthus caudatus*	Love-lies-bleeding, velvet flower, tassel flower, prince's feather	S. America
1596	Anemone coronaria	Windflower	S. Europe
1596	Campanula pyramidalis*	Chimney bellflower, steeple bellflower	Italy, Yugoslavia
1596	Hyacinthus orientalis*	Jacinths, common hyacinth	C. & S. Turkey, Syria, Lebanon
1596	Narcissus jonquilla*	Junquils, jonquils	Spain, Portugal
1596	Nerium oleander	Bay Rose, oleander	Mediterranean
1596	Primula auricula*	Bear's ears, auricula	Alps
1596	Ranunculus*		
1597	Citrus limon	Lemon	
1597	Citrus sinensis	Sweet orange	
c.1597	Hibiscus rosa-sinensis		Tropical Asia
1597	Lytocaryum weddellianum	Cocos palm	SE. Brazil, W. Europe to E. Asia
1600s	Cyclamen persicum		E. Mediterranean
1629	Helichrysum stoechas	Immortalle, Everlasting flower	W. Mediterranean
1629	Polianthes tuberosa*	Tuberose	S. America
1631	Pelargonium triste		Cape
1637	Mimosa pudica	Sensitive plant, humble plant	S. America
1690	Ficus benghalensis	Banyan tree, Indian fig tree	India
1692	Agapanthus africans		South Africa
1700s	Caladium bicolour		Brazil
1701	Pelargonium capitatum		South Africa (Cape)
1701	Pelargonium peltatum	Ivy-leafed geranium	South Africa (Cape)
1703	Fuchsia triphylla		S. America and W. Indies
1710	Pelargonium zonale	Geranium	South Africa (Cape)
1712	Amaryllis belladonna	Belladonna lily	South Africa (Cape)
1714	Pelargonium inquinans		South Africa (Cape)
1720	Aloe variegata		South Africa
1721	Ficus pumila	Creeping fig, climbing fig, dwarf fig-tree	India
1723	Pelargonium fulgidum		South Africa (Cape)

Plants introduced or discovered between 1730 and 1840

Date	Botanical name	Common name, Historical name	Country or area of origin if known
1730	Aloe arborescens	Scarlet African aloe	
1730	Aloe glauca	Grey aloe	
1730	Aloe humilis	Spider aloe, hedgehog aloe, crocodile aloe	South Africa (Cape)
1730	Aloe variegata	Spotted aloe	
1731	Chamaeops humilis	Dwarf palm, palmetto	
1731	Ficus religiosa	Bo tree, sacred fig	India
1731	Opuntia ficus-indica	Bunny's ear cactus, Indian fig	Mexico
1735	Heliotrope peruvianum	Cherry pie	Peru
1739	Crassula arborescens	Jade plant, money tree	South Africa
1739	Camellia japonica		E. Asia
1739	Peperomia obtusifolium	Baby rubber plant, radiator plant	
1750	Tradescantia spathacea	Moses-in-the-cradle, boat lily, oyster plant, Moses-in-the-bullrushes	America
1752	Reseda odorata	Frenchman's darling, little darling, fragrant weed, mignonette	
1754	Gardenia augusta	Cape jessamine, jasmin	China
1757	Heliotropium arborescens	Cherry pie, heliotrope	Peru
1759	Ficus benjamina	Weeping fig, Benjamin tree	India
1760s	Dracaena fragrans	Corn lily	C. & E. Asia
1764	Solenostemon scutellarioides	Coleus, painted nettle	New Guinea
1767	Bougainvillea		Brazil
1770	Cordyline terminalis	Ti plant	C. & E. Asia
1771	Cordyline fruticosa		China
1773	Strelizia reginae	Bird of paradise	South Africa
1774	Plectranthus fruticosus	Coleus var.	South Africa
1775	Encephalartos alternsteinii	Sourberg cycad	South Africa (Cape)
1777	Calceolaria fothergillii	Fothergill's slipper flower	Falkland Is./Patagonia
1780s	Phormium tenax variegata	New Zealand flax	New Zealand
1781	Cyperus alternifolius	Umbrella plant	Madagascar
1783	Aucuba japonica	Spotted laurel	Japan
1786	Ficus microcarpa	Indian laurel, curtain fig, Malay banyan	India
1787	Erica gentricosa	Cape heather	South Africa (Cape)
1788	Chlorophytum orchidastrum	Spider plant	Japan
1788	Fuchsia coccinea		Chile
1789	Ficus rubiginosa	Rusty fig, little-leaf fig, Port Jackson fig	Australia
1789	Hydrangea macrophylla		Japan, Korea
1790	Cissus antarctica	Grape vine, kangaroo vine	Australia
1790	Sparmannia africanana	African hemp, house lime	South Africa
1793	Adiantum macrophyllum	Large-leaf maidenhair	W. Indies

Date	Botanical name	Common name, Historical name	Country or area of origin if known
1793	*Adiantum tenerum*	Maidenhair fern	W. Indies
1793	*Adiantum trapeziforme*	Giant maidenhair fern, diamond maidenhair fern	W. Indies
1793	*Araucaria heterophylla*	Norfolk Island pine, House Pine	Australia
1793	*Fuchsia magellanica*		Chile, Peru
1793	*Lygodium microphyllum*	Climbing fern	E. Indies
1793	*Nephrolepis exaltata* 'Bostoniensis'	Boston fern	Tropics
1793	*Peperomia magnoliaefolium*	Desert privet	
1794	*Commeliana benghalensis*	Widow's tears, day flower	C. & E. Asia
1808	*Platycerium bifurcatum*	Common staghorn fern	Australia
1810	*Codiaeum variegatum* var. *pictum*	Croton	Papuasia, W. Pacific
1811	*Lithops*	Living stones, pebble plants	Cape
1814	*Begonia corallina*		Brazil
1815	*Ficus elastica*	Rubber plant, India rubber tree	India
1815	*Sinningia speciosa*	Florists' gloxinia	Tropical Brazil
1818	*Plumbago auriculata*	Cape leadwort	South Africa
1820s	*Calceolaria cana*		Chile
1820s	*Clivia*	Kaffir lily	South Africa
1821	*Primula sinensis*	Chinese primrose	C. & E. Asia
1822	*Calceolaria corymbosa*	Slipper flower, slipperwort, pocketbook flower, pouch flower	Chile
1822	*Calceolaria integrifolia*	Lady's slipper	Chile
1822	*Dracaena surculosa*	Gold dust dracaena, spotted dracaena	
1822	*Streptocarpus rexii*	Cape primrose	Cape
1823	*Aspidistra elatior*	Cast-iron plant, bar-room plant	China
1827–69	*Aloe aristata*	Torch plant, lace aloe	Cape
1827–69	*Cotyledon undulata*	Silver crown, silver ruffles	Cape
1827–69	*Haworthia reinwardtii*		Cape
1827–69	*Haworthia venosa* subsp. *tesselata*		Cape
1829	*Bougainvillea spectabilis*		S. America
1833	*Rhododendron simsii*	Indian azalea	C. & E. Asia
1834	*Euphorbia pulcherrima*	Poinsettia, lobster plant, Christmas star	South Africa
1834	*Tradescantia fluminensis*	Wandering Jew, inch plant	Argentina/Brazil
1836	*Aeschynanthus parasiticus*	Lipstick plant, basket vine	India
1836	*Rhododendron formosum*		India
1837	*Cephalocereus senilis*	Old man cactus	Mexico
1839	*Pericallis* x *hybrida*	Florists' cineraria	Canary Islands
1839	*Stephanotis floribunda*	Madagascar jasmine, floradora, bridal wreath, wax flower	Madagascar

Plants introduced or discovered between 1840 and 1900

Date	Botanical name	Common name / Historical name	Country or area of origin if known
1840s	*Fuchsia fulgens*		Guatemala
1840s	*Hoya lanceolata* subsp. *bella*	Miniature wax plant	SE. Asia
1840s	*Medinilla magnifica*	Rose grape	SE. Asia
1841	*Ficus lutea*	Lagos rubber tree, Zulu fig	Tropical & South Africa
1843	*Begonia fuchsioides*	Fuchsia begonia	
1843	*Episcia cupreata*		Colombia, Venezuela, Brazil
1843	*Ruellia macrantha*	Christmas pride	Brazil
1845	*Aphelandra aurantiaca*	Fiery spike	Mexico, Colombia
1845	*Calathea villosa* var. *pardina*		Brazil, Venezuela
1845	*Calathea metallica*		Colombia, Brazil
1845–7	*Aeschynanthus speciosus*		SE. Asia
1845–6	*Begonia coccinea*	Angel-wing begonia	Brazil
1846	*Calathea makoyana*	Peacock plant, cathedral windows	E. Brazil
1850s–60s	*Achimenes grandiflora*	Hot water plant	Mexico
1853–5	*Streptocarpus gardenii*		E. Cape/Natal
1853–5	*Streptocarpus polyanthus*		Transvaal, Orange Free State, Natal
1850	*Tradescantia zebrina*		Mexico
1857	*Dianthus* 'Souvenir de la Malmaison'	Malmaison carnation	France
1858	*Begonia rex*	King begonia, painted-leaf begonia	India/Himalaya/Assam
1858	*Caladium humboldtii*	Angel wings, elephant's ears	Brazil/Venezuela
1860	*Aglaonema commutatum*	Chinese evergreen	Tropical Asia
1861	*Begonia strigillosa*		Guatemala, Costa Rica
1862	*Calathea veitchiana*		Peru
1862	*Alocasia lowii*	Elephant's ear	Borneo
1863	*Aspidistra punctata*	Cast-iron plant	China
1863	*Hippeastrum leopoldii*		Bolivia
1863	*Saxifraga fortunei*		Japan
1863	*Sanchezia speciosa*	Shrubby whitevein	Ecuador, Peru
1864	*Ficus aspera* 'Parcellii'	Clown fig, Mosaic fig	Tropics
1865	*Begonia boliviensis*		S. America
1865	*Oplismenus hirtellus*	Bristle basketgrass	Tropical Africa, America, Polynesia
1865	*Schefflera elegantissima*	False aralia	New Caledonia
1865	*Schefflera veitchii*		New Caledonia
1865–8	*Pandanus veitchii*	Screw pine	SE. Asia
1866	*Dieffenbachia bowmanii*	Dumb cane	E. Brazil
1866	*Peperomia argyreia*	Rugby football plant, watermelon begonia	Northern S. America to Brazil

Date	Botanical name	Common name *Historical name*	Country or area of origin if known
1867	*Acalypha wilkesiana*	Copperleaf, beefsteak plant	Pacific Islands
1867	*Colocasia affinis*	Elephant's ear plant	Tropical E. Himalaya
1867	*Fittonia albivenis*	Mosaic plant, painted net leaf	Peru
1869	*Howea forsteriana*	Kentia palm	Lord Howe Island, Australia
1870s	*Philodendron melanochrysom*	Black-gold philodendron	Colombia
1872	*Dieffenbachia seguine* var. *liturata*	Dumb cane	
1872	*Dracaena goldieana*	Lucky bamboo	W. & C. Africa
1872	*Spathiphyllum wallisii*	Peace lily	Panama, Costa Rica
1873	*Bromelia balansae*	Heart of flame	South America
1875	*Maranta leuconeura*	Prayer plant, ten commandments	Brazil
1876	*Anthurium andraeanum*	Painter's palette, flamingo plant, tailflower plant	Colombia, Ecuador
1878	*Begonia decora*	Hairy begonia	Malaysia, Indochina
1878	*Hypoestes phyllostachya*	Polkadot plant, measles plant, freckle face, pink dot	South Africa, Madagascar, SE. Asia
1878	*Selaginella kruassiana*	Spreading club moss	South Africa
1879	*Primula obconica*	German primrose, poison primrose	China
1881	*Exacum affine*	Persian violet, German violet	S. Yemen
1892	*Dracaena sanderiana*	Ribbon plant, Belgian evergreen	Cameroon

ENDNOTES

INTRODUCTION
1 Platt, Sir Hugh, *Floraes Paradise* (1608), p. 31.
2 Ibid., pp. 30–1.
3 Lemnius, Levinus, 'Notes on England' (1560), in Rye, William Brenchley (ed.), *England as Seen by Foreigners* (1865), p. 80.
4 Power, Eileen (ed.), *The Goodman of Paris* (1928), pp. 203–4.

CHAPTER 1
'A GARDEN WITHIN DOORES'
1 Platt, pp. 30–1.
2 Ibid., pp. 34–5.
3 Ibid., pp. 35–6.
4 Ibid., pp. 37–8.
5 Lemnius, pp. 78–9.
6 Harrison, William, 'An historicall description of the island of Britayne, etc' (1577), in Holinshed, R., *The Firste volume of the Chronicles of England*, etc, (1807), I, p. 85.
7 Markham, Gervase, *The Second Booke of the English Husbandman* (1635), p. 6.
8 Lawson, William, *A New Orchard and Garden* (1618), in Roberts, Judith, 'The gardens of the gentry in the late Tudor period', *Garden History* (1999), 27, 1, p. 94.
9 *A Book of Fruits and Flowers* (1653), p. 7.
10 Cavendish, George, *The Life of Cardinal Wolsey*, (1825) 1, p. 43.
11 Braithwait, R., *Some Rules and Orders for the Government of the House of an Earles* (1624), in Henderson, Paula, *The Tudor House and Garden* (2005), p. 116.
12 Tusser, Thomas, *Five Hundred Points of Good Husbandry* (1573), p. 69.

CHAPTER 2
THE ARRIVAL OF 'EXOTICKS'
1 Gerard[e], John, *The Herball, or Generall Historie of Plantes* (1597).
2 Quoted in Hughes, G. Bernard, 'Georgian pots for flowers and bulbs', *Country Life*, 7 March 1963, p. 490.
3 Parkinson, John, *Paradisi in sole paradisus terrestris* (1629), p. 346.
4 Ibid., p. 430.
5 Quoted in MacGregor, Arthur, 'Tradescant, John, the younger (*bap.* 1608, *d.* 1662), *ODNB*.

6 Quoted in Woods, May and A. Warren, *Glasshouses: A History of Greenhouses, Orangeries and Conservatories* (1988), p. 10.
7 Ibid., pp. 10–11.
8 Rea, John, *Flora* (1665), p. 16.
9 Worlidge, John, *Systema Horti-culturae* (1677), p. 4.
10 Parkinson, p. 258.
11 Manning, Anne, *Mary Powell and Deborah's Diary* (1908), p. 128.
12 Worlidge, p. 4.
13 Platt, p. 105.
14 Parkinson, p. 369.
15 Hanbury, Revd William, *A Complete Body of Planting and Gardening* (1770), in Coats, Alice, *Flowers and their Histories* (1956), p. 136.
16 Parkinson, p. 584.
17 Evelyn, John, *Kalendarium Hortense: or, The Gard'ners Almanac* (1664:1983), p. 64.
18 Quoted in Laird, Mark, 'Sayes Court revisited', in Harris, F. and M. Hunter (eds), *John Evelyn and his Milieu: Essays* (2003), p. 115.
19 Worlidge, p. 171.
20 Chambers, D., 'John Evelyn and the invention of the heated greenhouse,' *Garden History*, 20, 2 (1992), p. 201.
21 Fiennes, Celia, *Through England on a Side Saddle in the Reign of William and Mary* (1888), pp. 97–8.
22 Ibid., p. 26.
23 Ibid., p. 28.

CHAPTER 3
THE CHAMBER GARDEN
1 Fairchild, Thomas, *The City Gardener* (1722), p. 7.
2 Lucas, J. (ed.), *Kalm's Account of his Visit to England on his way to America in 1748* (1892), p. 85.
3 Fairchild, p. 63.
4 Quoted in Chambers, Douglas, '"Storys of Plants": The assembling of Mary Capel Somerset's botanical collection at Badminton', *Journal of the History of Collecting* (1997), 9, 1, p. 50.
5 Switzer, Stephen, *The Nobleman, Gentleman and Gardener's Recreation, or an introduction to gardening, planting, agriculture, etc.* (1715), p. 54.

6 Chambers, '"Storys of Plants"', pp. 52–3.
7 Ibid., p. 58.
8 Fairchild, p. 64.
9 London, George, and Henry Wise, *The Retir'd Gard'ner in two vols. Being a Translation of Le Jardinier Solitaire* [by F. Gentil] (1706), p. 393.
10 Fairchild, p. 64.
11 Ibid., p. 64.
12 Ibid., p. 65.
13 Meager, Leonard, *The English Gardener* (1688), p. 137.
14 Langley, Batty, *New Principles of Gardening, or the laying-out and planting Parterres* (1728).
15 Ibid., p. 187.
16 Ibid., p. 188.
17 Ibid.
18 Parkinson, pp. 9–10.

CHAPTER 4
THE FASHION FOR FORCING
1 Quoted in Duthie, Ruth, *Florists' Flowers and Societies* (1988), p. 15.
2 Fairchild, p. 60.
3 Climenson, Emily J. (ed.), *Passages from the Diaries of Mrs Philip Lybbe Powys* (1899), p. 116.
4 More, Sir Thom[as], Bart, 'A Flower-Garden for Gentlemen and Ladies', in Furber, Robert, *The Flower Garden Display'd* (1734, 2nd edition), p. 126.
5 Ibid., p. 132.
6 Ibid., pp. 126–7.
7 Ibid., pp. 127–8.
8 Ibid., p. 128.
9 Ibid., pp. 128–9.
10 Ibid., p. 132.
11 Ibid., pp. 133–4.
12 Ibid.
13 Ibid., p. 136.
14 London and Wise, p. 305–6.

CHAPTER 5
'PORCOPINS FOR SNOWDRIPS'
1 Delany, Mary, *The Autobiography and Correspondence of Mary Granville, Mrs. Delany*, 2 (1879), 14 September 1772.
2 Hibbert, C. (ed.), *An American in Regency England: The Journal of a Tour in 1810–11* (1968), p. 54.
3 Delany, 7 June 1774.
4 Wedgwood, Josiah, 'Commonplace book 1', Wedgwood Archive (WA).
5 Ibid.
6 Wedgwood, Josiah, *Letters*, VI (1772), 5

August 1772, Wedgwood Museum Trust.
7 Ibid.
8 Wedgwood, *Letters*, 15 August 1772.
9 Wedgwood, *Letters*, 13 September 1772.
10 WA, catalogue, 1787.
11 Ibid.
12 Wedgwood, *Letters*, II, 31 December 1767.
13 Coats, p. 111.
14 Coke, Lady Mary Campbell, 'Diary of Lady Mary Campbell Coke, September 1767', in *The Letters and Journals of Lady Mary Coke, vol. 2* (1889), p. 440.
15 Phillips, Henry, *Flora Historica*, 2 (1829), p. 143.
16 Hibbert, p. 54.
17 *Transactions of the Horticultural Society*, II, p. 374, read July 1 1817.
18 WA, Mss E53–30014.
19 Haworth, Adrian Hardy, 'On the cultivation of crocuses' (read 7 February, 1809), *Transactions of the Horticultural Society of London*, XXII (1820), pp. 122–31.
20 Anon., *Low-Life: or One Half of the World, Knows not how the Other Half Lives* (1752:1764), p. 27.

CHAPTER 6
TOWN AND VILLA
1 Lemmon (1962), p. 126.
2 Repton, Humphry, Observations on the theory and practice of landscape gardening (1803), p. 105.
3 Bradley, Dr Richard, *The Gentleman and Gardener's Kalendar* (1718), quoted in Woods and Warren, p. 56.
4 Repton, Humphry, *Fragments on the Theory of Landscape Gardening* (1816), p. 28.
5 Tod, George, *Tod's Plans of Hot-Houses, Green-Houses, An Aquarium, Conservatories, &c. recently built in different parts of England for Various Noblemen and Gentlemen* (1807).
6 Tod, *Plans*, Plate IX, p. 14.
7 Quoted in Willson, E.J., *James Lee and the Vineyard Nursery* Hammersmith (Hammersmith Local History Group, 1961), p. 29.
8 Loudon, J.C., *Encyclopaedia of Gardening* (1822), 1039.
9 Loudon, J.C., *Green-house Companion* (1824), pp. 241–2.
10 Ibid., pp. 244–5.
11 Nicol, Walter, *The Villa Garden Directory* (1810), pp. 356–7.

12   Ibid., p. 357–8.
13   Loudon, *Green-house*, pp. 246–7.
14   Cruikshank, I.M. 'The Corinthian Capital', aquatint from Pierce Egan, *Life in London* (1823).
15   Ibid., pp. 248–9.
16   Mangles, James, *The Floral Calendar* (1839), p. iv.
17   Ibid., pp. 70–1.

CHAPTER 7
'THE LARGEST HOT–HOUSE IN THE WORLD'
1   *Gardener's Magazine*, 5 (1829), p. 684.
2   Ward, N.B., *On the Growth of Plants in Closely Glazed Cases* (1852), p. 37.
3   Quoted in Solman, David, *Loddiges of Hackney: The Largest Hothouse in the World* (1995), p. 44.
4   Loudon, J.C., 'Growing ferns and other plants in glass cases', *Gardener's Magazine*, 10, pp. 162–3.
5   Mangles, pp. 93–4.
6   Ibid., p. 93.
7   Harvey, John, *Early Nurserymen* (1974), p. 89.
8   'Calls at London nurseries: The Hackney Botanic Garden', *Gardener's Magazine* (1833), 9, p. 467.
9   Solman, p. 39.
10   Chapman-Huston, Desmond and E. Cripps, *Through a City Archway: The Story of Allen and Hanbury's 1715–1954* (1954), p. 279, quoted in Solman, pp. 35–6.
11   *Ladies' Magazine of Gardening* (1842), p. 51.
12   Ibid.
13   Ibid., p. 45.
14   Quoted in Solman, p. 42.

CHAPTER 8
FLORA DOMESTICA
1   Kent, Elizabeth, *Flora Domestica* (1823), p. xiii.
2   Ibid., pp. xxxiii–iv.
3   *Ladies' Magazine*, pp. 60–1.
4   *Gentleman's Magazine*, 71, 1 (1801), pp. 199–200.
5   Johnson, Louisa, *Every Lady's Guide to her own Greenhouse, Hothouse and Conservatory* (1851), p. 3.
6   Ibid., p. 4.
7   Loudon, Jane, *The Ladies' Flower-Garden of Ornamental Greenhouse Plants* (1848), p. 1.
8   *The Housekeeper's Receipt Book or, The Repository of Domestic Knowledge* (1813), p. 324.
9   Mangles, p. 47.
10   Loudon, Mrs, *Gardening for Ladies* (1846), p. 381.
11   Beeton, Isabella, *The Book of Household Management* (1861:2000), p. 561.
12   *Ladies' Magazine* (1841), p. 213.
13   *Gentleman's Magazine*, 34 (1764), p. 207.
14   Quoted in Longstaffe-Gowan, R. Todd, 'Plant Effluvia: Changing notions of the effects of plant exhalations on human health in the eighteenth and nineteenth centuries', *Journal of Garden History*, 7, 2, p. 176.
15   *Ladies' Magazine*, p. 213.
16   Nightingale, Florence, *Notes on Nursing* (1859), p. 84.
17   *Ladies' Magazine*, p. 148.
18   Loudon, *Ladies' Flower-Garden*, p. 1.
19   Loudon, Mrs, *The Lady's Country Companion* (1845), p. 18.
20   Kent, p. 166.

CHAPTER 9
RUS IN URBE
1   Haweis, Mrs, *The Art of Decoration* (1881), p. 358.
2   Hibberd, Shirley, *Rustic Adornments for Homes of Taste* (1856), pp. vi–xi.
3   Ibid., pp. 2–3.
4   *Ladies' Magazine*, pp. 278–9.
5   Hibberd, *Rustic*, p.150.
6   Kingsley, Charles, *Glaucus* (1855), p. 4.
7   Allen, D.E., *The Victorian Fern Craze* (1969), pp. 70–1.
8   Hassard, Annie, *Floral Decorations for Dwelling Houses* (1876), p. 134.
9   Maling, E.A., *In-door Plants & How to Grow Them* (1862), p. 68.
10   *The Garden*, 7 Sept 1873, p. 208.
11   Maling, p. 62.
12   *Journal of Horticulture and Cottage Gardener*, 13 May 1875, p. 365.
13   Maling, p. 83.
14   Burbidge, F.W.T., *Domestic Floriculture* (18743), pp. 64–5.
15   Hibberd, *Rustic*, pp. 160–1.
16   *The Garden*, 25 November 1871, p. 5.
17   Ibid., 2 December 1871, p. 43.
18   Ibid., 31 Jan 1874, p. 96.
19   Ibid., p. 97.
20   Burbidge, p. 10.
21   Maling, p. 73.
22   Ibid., p. 22.

CHAPTER 10
GARDENS UNDER GLASS

1　Hibberd, Shirley, *The Amateur's Greenhouse and Conservatory* (1888), p. 53.
2　Yonge, Charlotte, *The Daisy Chain, or Aspirations* (1856), Chapter 15, quoted in Michael Waters, 'The Conservatory in Victorian Literature', *Journal of Garden History* (1982), 2, 3, p. 276.
3　Ibid., p. 280.
4　Gardener's Magazine (1836), p. 293.
5　Knight's *Cyclopaedia of London* (c. 1851), quoted in Boniface, Patricia, *The Garden Room* (1982), p. iii.
6　Quoted in Woods, p. 167.
7　Robinson, William, *Parks, Promenades & Gardens of Paris* (1869), p. 280.
8　Hibberd, *Amateur*, p. 218.
9　March, T.C., *Flower and Fruit Decoration* (1862), p. 92.
10　Ibid., pp. 92–4.
11　Ibid.
12　Hibberd, *Amateur*, p. 267.
13　Hibberd, Shirley, *New and Rare Beautiful-leaved Plants* (1870), pp. 89–92.
14　*Gardeners' Chronicle*, 8 June 1861, p. 531.
15　*Floral Magazine* (1862), Plate 96.
16　*Gardeners' Chronicle*, 21 November 1868, p. 1210.
17　Ibid., p. 92.
18　Veitch, James, *Hortus Veitchii* (1906), p. 265.
19　*Gardeners' Chronicle*, 21 November 1868, p. 208.
20　Hibberd, *New and Rare*, p. 5.
21　Ibid., p. 106.
22　Loudon, *Encyclopaedia*, p. 1224.
23　March, p. 84.
24　Ibid., p. 69.

CHAPTER 11
WINDOW GARDENS
FOR THE PEOPLE

1　Dickens, Charles, *The Pickwick Papers*, Chapter 42.
2　Buckton, Catherine, *Town and Window Gardening* (1879), p. viii.
3　Ibid., p. x.
4　Ibid., p. v.
5　Ibid., pp. 136–149.
6　Ibid.
7　Parkes, Revd S.H., *Window Gardens for the People and clean and tidy rooms, being an experiment to improve the homes of the London Poor* (1864), p. 30.

8　*The Day of Rest* (September 1865), p. 458, quoted in Matheson, Julia. '"A New Gleam of Social Sunshine": Window Garden Flower Shows for the Working Classes 1860–1875', *The London Gardener*, 9 (2003–4), p. 63.
9　Parkes, pp. 32–3.
10　*Gardeners' Chronicle*, 23 July 1864, p. 678.
11　Parkes, p. 50.
12　Ibid., pp. 50–1.
13　*The Times*, 9 July 1866, p. 12.
14　*Gardener's Magazine*, 13 April 1867, p. 151.
15　Quoted in Duthie, p. 27.
16　Ibid., p. 31.
17　Parkes, Revd S. Hadden, *Flower Shows of Window Plants for the Working Classes of London* (Victoria Press, 1862), pp. 5–6, quoted in Julia Matheson, '" It really is a wery pretty garden": Popular gardening in London 1860–1900, with particular reference to Floricultural Societies and their shows in Tower Hamlets and the Window Gardening for the Poor Movement;, unpublished MA dissertation (Open University, 2001), p. 5.
18　Glenny's *Gardener's Gazette*, June 1862, p. 133, quoted in Julia Matheson, (2010). Common ground: horticulture and the cultivation of open space in the East End of London, 1840–1900. PhD thesis, The Open University.
19　*East London Observer*, 24 November 1866, p. 2, quoted in Matheson, pp. 12–13.
20　Ibid., p. 14.
21　Wright, Walter P., 'Gardening in London' in *Living London*, 1 (Cassell, 1903), p. 307, quoted in Matheson, pp. 14–15.
22　*Gardener's Magazine* 26 May 1866, p. 234.
23　Quoted in Long, Helen, *The Edwardian House* (1993), p. 45.

CHAPTER 12
FLOWER DECORATIONS

1　Quoted in Pevsner, Nikolaus, *Pioneers of Modern Design* (1966), p. 148.
2　Jekyll, Gertrude, *Flower Decoration in the House* (1907:1982), p. 106.
3　Ibid., p. 132.
4　Ibid., pp. 126–9.
5　Ibid., pp. 130–1.
6　Ibid., p. 107.
7　Earle, Mrs, *Pot-Pourri from a Surrey Garden* (1897:2004), p. 20.

8   Ibid., p. 23.
9   Ibid., p. 21.
10   Spry, Constance, *Flower Decoration*
     (1934), p. 92.
11   'Plants Indoors', A Special Number of
     the *Architectural Review*, CXI, 665 (May
     1952), p. 295.

CHAPTER 13
'NO HOME IS COMPLETE
WITHOUT LIVING PLANTS'
1   Ibid., p. 295.
2   Lancaster, Osbert, *A Cartoon History of
     Architecture* (1959:1975), p. 178.
3   Flanders, Michael and Donald Swann,
     'Design for Living' from *At the Drop of a
     Hat* (1956).
4   Correspondence with author, 2005.
5   Stevenson, Violet, 'The return of the
     potted plant', *Country Life*, 8 February
     1952, p. 350.
6   *The Journal of The Saintpaulia &
     Houseplant Society,* 2002, p. 2.
7   Lancaster, p. 180.
8   Ibid.
9   Davidson, William, *Woman's Own Book of
     House Plants* (1969), p. 15.
10   Ibid., p. 18.

CHAPTER 14
'GOOD FOR YOUR HEALTH AND
GOOD FOR YOUR SOUL'
1   Sturgeon, Andy, *Potted* (2001), p. 7.
2   Correspondence with author, 2005.
3   *The Sunday Times Style* magazine,
     24 November 2019, p. 11.

CONCLUSION
1   Figures from the RHS, released 8 October
     2019, of Ipsos Mori survey conducted in
     March 2019.
2   Hancock, Alice 'House plants enjoy a
     growth spurt of popularity', *Financial
     Times*, 27 April 2018, retrieved
     28 April 2018.
3   *The Garden*, November 2019, p. 6.
4   Hancock, 'House plants'; Moshakis, Alex,
     'House plants: The new bloom economy',
     The Observer, 30 June 2019; Boyle,
     Matthew, 'The one thing millennials
     haven't killed is houseplants', *Bloomberg*,
     11 April 2019, retrieved 12 December
     2019.

5   Wilson, Matthew, *Financial Times*,
     12 September 2014, retrieved 30 October
     2018.
6   Hotten, Russell, 'The future of food:
     Why farming is moving indoors', https://
     www.bbc.co.uk/news/business-49052317,
     retrieved 11 December 2019.
7   https://www.theguardian.com/
     global/2019/jun/30/house-plants-bloom-
     economy-wellbeing
     retrieved 9 September 2019.
8   Email correspondence with author, 2019.
9   Press release, RHS, 'RHS grows houseplant
     and floristry offering as indoor gardening
     blooms', 8 October 2019.
10   https://www.theguardian.com/
     lifeandstyle/2020/jan/15/plants-is-it-ok-
     to-steal-cuttings, retrieved 16 January
     2020.
11   https://planthealthportal.defra.gov.uk/
     plant-biosecurity-strategy/, retrieved 11
     December 2019.
12   Correspondence with author, 2020.
     See also https://www.researchgate.net/
     publication/333450759_Plants_as_a_
     building_service_Improving_indoor_
     air_quality_and_reducing_energy_
     consumption_-a_critical_review,
     retrieved 21 January 2020.
13   Correspondence with author, 2019.
14   https://www.telegraph.co.uk/gardening/
     how-to-grow/millennials-risk-killing-
     houseplant-obsession-created/, retrieved
     19 October 2019.

BIBLIOGRAPHY

In addition to the many primary sources mentioned in the notes, I have used a wide variety of other books and articles in my research. This is a selected list loosely divided into centuries together with some essential reading on general topics.

For this new revised edition, helpful social media and website addresses have also been included.

GENERAL

Bennett, Sue, *Five Centuries of Women & Gardens* (National Portrait Gallery, 2001)
Blacker, Mary Rose, *Flora Domestica: A History of Flower Arranging 1500–1930* (National Trust, 2000)
Boniface, Patricia, *The Garden Room* (HMSO,1982)
Campbell-Culver, Maggie, *The Origin of Plants* (Eden Project Books, 2001)
Fisher, John, *The Origins of Garden Plants* (Constable, 1982)
Gordon, Lesley, *Poorman's Nosegay: Flowers from a Cottage Garden* (Collins, 1973)
Grimshaw, Dr John, *The Gardener's Atlas* (Firefly, 2002)
Hobhouse, Penelope, *Plants in Garden History* (Pavilion, 1992)
Huxley, Anthony (ed.), *The World Guide to House Plants* (Macmillan, 1983)
Kingsbury, Noel, *The Indoor Gardener* (Headline, 1994)
Lemmon, Kenneth, *The Covered Garden* (Museum Press, 1962)
Musgrave, Toby, Chris Gardner and Will Musgrave, *The Plant Hunters* (Ward Lock, 1999)
Quest-Ritson, Charles, *The English Garden: A Social History* (Viking, 2001)
Snodin, Michael, and J. Styles, *Design and the Decorative Arts: Britain 1500–1900* (V&A, 2001)
Tergit, Gabriele, *Flowers through the Ages* (Charles Skilton, 1972)
Thornton, Peter, *Authentic Décor: The Domestic Interior 1620–1920* (Weidenfeld & Nicolson, 1984)
Webber, Ronald, *Market Gardening: The History of Commercial Flower, Fruit and Vegetable Growing* (David & Charles, 1972)
Woods, May, and Arete Warren, *Glasshouses: A History of Greenhouses, Orangeries and Conservatories* (Aurum Press, 1988)

SIXTEENTH AND SEVENTEENTH CENTURY

Black, Virginia, 'Beddington – "the best Orangery in England"', *Journal of Garden History* (1983,) 3, 2, pp. 113–20
Chambers, Douglas, '"Storys of Plants": The assembling of Mary Capel Somerset's botanical collection at Badminton', *Journal of the History of Collecting* (1997), 9, 1, pp. 49–60
Cottesloe, Gloria, *The Duchess of Beaufort's Flowers* (Exeter, 1983)
Duthie, Ruth, *Florists' Flowers and Societies* (Shire, 1988)
Harvey, John, *Early Gardening Catalogues* (Phillimore, 1972)
-----, *Early Nurserymen* (Phillimore, 1974)
-----, 'The English nursery flora, 1677–1723', *Garden History* (1998), pp. 60–101
Henderson, Paula, *The Tudor House and Garden* (Yale University Press, 2005)
Henrey, Blanche, *British Botanical and Horticultural Literature before 1800* (Oxford University Press, 1975)
Laird, Mark, 'Sayes Court revisited', in F. Harris and M. Hunter (eds), *John Evelyn and his Milieu: Essays* (British Library, 2001)
Pollock, Linda, *With Faith and Physic: The Life of a Tudor Gentlewoman, Lady Grace Mildmay 1552–1620* (Collins & Brown, 1993)
Riddell, John, 'John Parkinson's Long Acre garden 1600–1650', *Journal of Garden History* (1986), 6, 2, pp. 112–124
Roberts, Judith, 'The gardens of the gentry in the late Tudor period,' *Garden History* (1999), 27, 1, pp. 89–208
Tolkowsky, Samuel, *Hesperis: A History of the Culture & Use of Citrus Fruits* (1938)

Vigarello, Georges, *Concepts of Cleanliness: Changing Attitudes in France since the Middle Ages* (Cambridge University Press, 1988)

Woudstra, Jan, 'The use of flowering plants in late seventeenth- and early eighteenth-century interiors', *Garden History* (2000), 28, 2, pp. 194–208

EIGHTEENTH CENTURY

Archer, Michael, *Delftware: The Tin-glazed Earthenware of the British Isles: A Catalogue in the Collection of the Victoria and Albert Museum* (V&A, 1997)

Ellis, Joyce, 'Georgian Town Gardens', *History Today* (January 2000)

Ferguson, Patricia, 'The eighteenth-century mania for hyacinths', *Antiques* (June 1997)

-----, 'Indoor gardening in the eighteenth century', *Antiques* (January 1999)

Girouard, Mark, *Life in the English Country House* (Penguin, 1980)

Greig, Hannah, 'Eighteenth-century English interiors in image and text,' in Jeremy Ansley and C. Grant (eds), *Imagined Interiors: Representing the Domestic Interior since the Renaissance* (V&A, 2006)

Guillery, Peter, *The Small House in Eighteenth-century London: A Social and Architectural History* (Yale University Press, 2004)

Hayden, Ruth, *Mrs Delany: Her Life and Her Flowers* (British Museum, 1980)

Harvey, John H., *The Availability of Hardy Plants of the Late Eighteenth Century* (Garden History Society, 1988)

Hughes, G. Bernard, 'Georgian pots for flowers and bulbs', *Country Life*, 7 March 1963, p. 490

Le Rougetel, Hazel, *The Chelsea Gardener: Philip Miller 1691–1771* (British Museum, 1990)

Leapman, Michael, *The Ingenious Mr Fairchild* (Headline, 2000)

Longstaffe Gowan, R. Todd, 'Plant Effluvia: Changing notions of the effects of plant exhalations on human health in the eighteen and nineteenth centuries', *Journal of Garden History*, 7, 2, pp. 176–85

-----, *The London Town Garden 1700–1840* (Yale University Press, 2001)

Plumb, J. H., *Georgian Delights* (Weidenfeld & Nicolson, 1980)

Schtier, Ann B., *Cultivating Women, Cultivating Science* (Johns Hopkins, 1996)

Webber, Ronald, *The Early Horticulturalists* (David & Charles, 1968)

-----, *Covent Garden:. Mud-salad Market* (Dent, 1969)

NINETEENTH CENTURY

Allen, David Elliston, *The Victorian Fern Craze: A History of Pteridomania* (Hutchinson, 1969)

Ashberry, Anne, *Bottle Gardens and Fern Cases* (Hodder & Stoughton, 1964)

Davies, Jennifer, *Saying It with Flowers: The Story of the Flower Shop* (Headline, 2000)

Elliott, Brent, 'Changing fashions in the conservatory', *Country Life*, 30 June 1983

Gere, Charlotte, *Nineteenth-century Decoration: The Art of the Interior* (Weidenfeld & Nicholson, 1989)

----, *Nineteenth-century Interiors: An Album of Watercolours* (Thames & Hudson, 1992)

Hansen, Eric, *Orchid Fever* (Methuen, 2001)

Laird, Mark, 'From bouquets to baskets', *Antiques* (June, 2000)

Longstaffe-Gowan, Todd, 'James Cochran: Florist and plant contractor to Regency London', *Journal of Garden History* (1987), 15, 1, pp. 55–63

Marshall, John, and I. Willox, *The Victorian House* (Sidgwick & Jackson, 1986)

Matheson, Julia, '"A New Gleam of Social Sunshine": Window garden fFlower shows for the working classes 1860–1875', *London Gardener*, 9 (2003–4), pp. 60–69

Scourse, Nicolette, *The Victorians and their Flowers* (Croom Helm, 1983)

Shephard, Sue, *Seeds of Fortune: A Gardening Dynasty* (Bloomsbury, 2003)

Solmon, David, *Loddiges of Hackney: The Largest Hothouse in the World* (Hackney Society, 1995)

Waters, Michael, *The Garden in Victorian Literature* (Scolar Press, 1988)

Whittingham, Sarah, *The Victorian Fern Craze* (Shire, 2009)

-----, *Fern Fever: The Story of Pteridomania* (Frances Lincoln, 2012)

Wilkinson, Anne, *Shirley Hibberd, the Father of Amateur Gardening: His Life and Works, 1825–1890* (Cortex Design, 2012)

TWENTIETH CENTURY

Allen, Mea, *Tom's Weeds: The Story of Rochford's & their House Plants* (Faber & Faber, 1970)

Banham, Reyner, *Guide to Modern Architecture* (Architectural Press, 1962)

Brookes, John, *The Indoor Garden Book* (Dorling Kindersley, 1986)

Hessayon, Dr D. G., *Be Your Own House Plant Expert* (Pan Britannic, 1960)

Jones, Margaret E., and H. F. Clark, *Indoor Plants and Gardens* (Architectural Press, 1952)

Lancaster, Osbert, *A Cartoon History of Architecture* (John Murray, 1959:1975)

Long, Helen, *The Edwardian House* (Manchester University Press, 1993)

Wolverton, Dr B. C., *How to Grow Fresh Air: 50 Houseplants that Purify Your Home or Office* (Penguin, 1997)

TWENTY-FIRST CENTURY

Bailey, Fran, *The Healing Power of Plants: The Hero House Plants that Love You Back* (Pop Press, 2019)

Carter, Hilton, *Wild at Home* (CICO Books, 2019)

Cheng, Darryl, *The New Plant Parent* (Abrams Image, 2019)

Colletti, Maria, *Living Decor: Plants, Potting and DIY Projects – Botanical Styling with Fiddle-Leaf Figs, Monsteras, Air Plants, Succulents, Ferns, and More of Your Favorite Houseplants* (Cool Springs Press, 2019)

Fowler, Alys, *Plant Love* (Kyle Books, 2018)

Hessayon, Dr D. G., *The Indoor Flower and House Plant Expert* (Pan Britannic, 2013)

Kassinger, Ruth, *Paradise under Glass* (William Morrow/HarperCollins, 2010)

Langton, Caro, and Rose Ray, *House of Plants: Living with Succulents, Air Plants and Cacti* (Frances Lincoln, 2016)

Leon, Gynelle, *Prick: Cacti and Succulents; Choosing, Styling and Caring* (Mitchell Beazley, 2017)

Oakes, Summer Rayne, *How to Make a Plant Love You: Cultivate Green Space in Your Home and Your Heart* (Penguin Random House, 2019)

Sibley, Emma, and Maaike Koster, *Urban Botanics: An Indoor Plant Guide for Modern Gardeners* (Aurum Press, 2017)

Southern, Nik, *How Not to Kill Your Plants* (Hodder & Stoughton, 2017)

Sturgeon, Andy, *Potted* (Conran Octopus, 2001)

A SELECTION OF POPULAR HOUSEPLANT RELATED
WEB AND SOCIAL MEDIA SITES

https://ebps.org.uk – (British Pteridological [Fern] Society – founded in 1891)

http://hortology.co.uk

https://janeperrone.com/on-the-ledge

https://national-begonia-society.co.uk

https://osgb.org.uk (Orchid Society of Great Britain)

https://patchplants.com

http://prickldn.com

https://scottishorchid.org

http://society.bcss.org.uk (British Cacti and Succulent Society)

https://streptocarpussociety.org.uk

https://thepags.org.uk (Pelargonium and Geranium Society)

https://thesill.com

https://ukaps.org (UK Aquatic Plant Society)

@aegarden
@botanygeek
@goodandplantiful
@hiltoncarter
@houseofhouseplantlovers
@houseplantguru
@houseplantjournal
@jamies_jungle
@j.l.perrone
@kingstreetjungle
@noughticulture

INDEX   Page references in **bold** are to plant lists

abutilon, 21
Acacia, 63
Acalypha wilkesiana, **159**
Achimenes, 96, 135, 144
   A. grandiflora, **158**
Adam, William Bridges, 97
Adiantum capillus-veneris,
   A. macrophyllum, **156**
   A. raddianum, 109, **156**
   A. tenerum, **157**
   A. trapeziforme, **157**
Aeschynanthus parasiticus, **157**
   A. speciosus, **158**
Africa, sculpture, 129
African marigold, 44
African violet.
   See Saintpaulia
Agapanthus africans, **155**
Agave, *A. americana*, **154**
Aglaonema commutatum, **158**
air pollution, 65, 66, 89–90,
   144–5, 152
air quality, 145
Alexandra, Princess of Wales, 109
Allen, D. E., 93
Allen, William, 74
Alocasia, 151
   A. lowii, **158**
   A. zebrina, 151
Aloe, 30, 31, 34
   A. arborescens, **156**
   A. aristata, **157**
   A. glauca, **156**
   A. humilis, **156**
   A. variegata, **155**, **156**
Aloysia triphylla, 53
Amaranthus, 44
   A. caudatus, **155**
   A. tricolor, **154**
Amaryllis belladonna, **155**
Amateur Gardening, 138
Amelia, Princess, 50
Amsterdam, 146
Anemone, 36, 37, 96, 119
   A. coronaria, **155**
Anne, Queen, 59, 146
Anthericum liliago variegatum,
   126
Anthurium andraeanum, **159**
   A. scherzerianum, 143
Antirrhinum majus, **154**
Aphelandra aurantiaca, **158**
apiaries, 91
aquaria, 92, 93, 102, 111
aquascaping, 93
Aquilegia vulgaris, 19, **154**
Aralia, 127
Araucaria, 127
   A. heterophylla, **157**
   A. excelsa 'Silver Star', 123

Arboretum, 81
Architectural Press, 137
Architectural Review, 129, 133
aristocracy, 31, 32, 61, 76, 113
Armacost & Royston, 136
Artemisia abrotanum, **154**
Arts and Crafts Exhibition
   (1888), 124
Arts and Crafts movement, 111
Asia, 24
Aspidistra, 110–11, 120, 124,
   126, 127, 144
   A. elatior, **157**
   A. punctata, 110, **158**
Asplenium nidus, 70
Assam, 107
aster, 117
Aucuba japonica, **156**
Auricula, 30, 36, 37, 39–40, 62,
   96, 118, 119
Austen, Jane,
   Northanger Abbey, 42
   Persuasion, 60
Australia, 69, 71, 110
aviaries, 102
Azaleas, 104, 135, 140

Baby Bio plant food, 138
Badminton House,
   Gloucestershire, 32
Bahamas, 75
balconies, 30, 50, 66, 79, 86,
   134, 150
balsams, 117
bamboo, 138
banana trees, 72
Banks, Sir Joseph, 49, 69, 76
Barbados lily, 32–3
Barnes, Surrey, 40
Bartram, John, 49
Bartram's boxes, 49, 69
Basil, 9, 19, 34
baskets, hanging, 97, 114, 115,
   138
Bassia scoparia
   f. tricholphylla, 26
Bateman, Richard, 54
Bath, 53
Bause, F., 105
Bay, 30, 39
Bazalgette, Sir Joseph, 89
BBC, 'Gardening Club', 137
Beaufort, Henry Somerset, 1st
   Duke of, 32
Beaufort, Henry Somerset, 2nd
   Duke of, 32
Beaufort, Mary Somerset,
   Duchess of, 31–3, 34, 76
Beaufortia, 32
Beckwith, George, 89

Beddington, Surrey, 22, 27
Bedford, Dukes of, 27
Bedford Conservatory, 109
Bedford Nursery, 55
Beeton, Elizabeth, 82, 84
Begon, Michael, 107
Begonia, 97, 107, 127, 144
   B. boliviensis, 107, **158**
   B. coccinea, 107, **158**
   B. corallina, **157**
   B. daedalea, 107
   B. davisii, 107
   B. decora, **159**
   B. falcifolia, 108
   B. fuchsioides, **158**
   B. masoniana, 144
   B. metallica, 125–6
   B. minor, 107
   B. pearcei, 107
   B. rex, **158**
   B. rexii, 107, 143
   B. strigillosa, **158**
   B. veitchiana, **158**
   B. veitchii, 107
Begoniaceae, 107
Belchier, William, 59
Belgium, 135
Bentinck, Hans William, 31
Bentley, Thomas, 51, 53, 56
Berlin, Royal Botanic Garden,
   136
Birkbeck, Emily G., 74
Birmingham, University of, 152
Blackett, Freddie, 150
Bletia purpurea, 75
Bolton,
   Albert Hall, 135
   Parks Department, 134
A Book of Fruits and Flowers, 18
botanical drawing, 81
Botanical Magazine, 106
botanists, 23, 30, 32, 34, 39,
   40, 42, 49, 54, 61–2, 69, 70,
   79–80, 107, 110, 151
botany, 75, 80–1, 85
'Botany Bens', 76
Bougainvillea, 137, **156**
   B. spectabilis, **157**
bough pots, 33, 51, 52–3, 93. *See
   also* containers
Bouvardias, 89
Box (Buxus), 16, 30
   B. sempervirens, 16, 34, **154**
Bradley, Richard, 60
   History of Succulent Plants,
   129
Brazil, 62, 75, 107
Breughel, Jan, the Elder, 24
Brexit, 152
briars, 17

British Cactus and Succulent Society, 151
British Streptocarpus Society, 151
Bromelia balansae, **159**
Broome, Samuel, 119
Brown, Lancelot 'Capability', 49, 60
Buckton, Catherine, 114–16, 119
Town and Window Gardening, 115
Buckton, Joseph, 114
bulb pots, 55
bulbs, 44–6, 63, 104, 128, 140
Bull, John, 110
Bull, William, 105–6, 108
Burbidge, Frederick, 94, 96, 98
Domestic Floriculture, 93–4
Burghley, Lord, 23, 26, 62, 75, 107
Burghley House, Lincolnshire, 26
Busch, Joseph, 72
Byng, Admiral John, 41

cachepots, 57, 95, 125, 140
Cacti, 127, 129, 137, 140
Caen, 18
Caladium, 125
C. bicolour, **155**
C. humboldtii, **158**
Calathea, 151
C. crocata, 143
C. makoyana, **158**
C. metallica, **158**
C. villosa var. *pardina*, **158**
Calceolaria, 96, 117
C. alba, 106
C. cana, **157**
C. corymbosa, **157**
C. fothergillii, **156**
C. integrifolia, **157**
Calcutta, 71
Callicoma serratifolia, 71
Calomeria amaranthoides, 146
Calthe veratrifolia, 73
Camellia, 11, 63, 74–5, 87, 102, 103, 104, 106, 124
C. japonica, 74, **156**
Campanula medium, 25
C. pyramidalis, 34, **155**
Canada, 69, 150
cannabis, 149
Canterbury bells, 25
Cape of Good Hope, 57, 105
Cape heathers, 49
Capell of Hadham, Arthur Capell, 1st Baron, 31
Capell of Tewkesbury, Henry Capell, 1st Baron, 31
Capsicum, 44
C. annum, **154**
Carew, Sir Francis, 22, 23, 27

Carnation.
See Dianthus caryophyllus
Carpets, 15, 16, 24, 49, 50, 66, 80, 93
Carter, Hilton, 150
catalogues, 26, 35, 41, 42, 73, 85, 94, 107, 111
Cattley, William, 75
Cattleya,
C. labiata, 75
C. loddigesii, 75
Cecil, William (later Lord Burghley), 23, 26, 62, 75, 107
Cecil family, 23
Celosia, 143
C. argentea var. *cristata*, **155**
centaurea, 22
Cephalocereus senilis, **157**
ceramics, horticultural, 51–3, 55
Chamaeops humilis, **156**
chamber garden, 29–37
Chapel Allerton, Yorkshire, 79
Charles I, King, 25
Charlotte, Queen, 41
Chatsworth House, Derbyshire, 73, 75
Great Conservatory, 127
Cheng, Darryl, 150
cherry trees, 66
Chile, 106
Chimney bellflower, 34
Chimonanthus fragrans, 126
China, 59, 72, 74, 110, 143
Chlorophytum,
C. comosum, 139, 145
C. orchidastrum, **156**
Chorizema cordata, 126
Christmas cactus, 140, 143
Chrysalidocarpus lutescens, 145
Chrysanthemum, 33, 116, 118, 119, 144
Cineraria, 104
Cissus antarctica, **156**
cities, living conditions, 115–16
Citrus, 22–3, 25, 26–7, 39, 103
'Meyer's Lemon', 143
C. aurantium, **155**
C. limon, **155**
C. mitis, 143
C. sinensis, **155**
Clean Air Act (1956), 133
Clianthus formosus, 31
Clivia, **157**
clothing fabrics, with floral motifs, 49–50
coal, 30, 59, 62–3, 65, 89, 98–9
fumes, 10, 35, 89–90
Cobham, Surrey, 126
Cochran, James, 65, 66–7, 140
Cockrell, Mr, 66
cockscomb, 44, 143

Codiaeum (croton), 102, 105, 107, 108, 125, 127, 130, 135
C. latimaculatus, 108
C. variegatum var. *pictum*, **157**
Coke, Lady Mary Campbell, 53
Coleus, 105–6, 135
C. bausei, 105
C. fruticosus, 105
C. marshallii, 106
C. murrayii, 106
C. telfordii aurea, 106
C. veitchii, 105
C. verschaffeltii, 105, 106
coleus fever, 105–6
Collinson, Peter, 49, 75
Colocasia affinis, **159**
colour, 124
colour schemes, 124
Columnea, 144
Colutea, 63
Colvill, James, 76–7
Comic Almanack, 80
Commeliana benghalensis, **157**
Compton, Henry, Bishop, 31
conduits, 29
Conran, Terence, 138
conservatories, 59–60, 86, 93, 95–6, 101–12, 125, 129, 138, 146
Constantinople, 31
containers, 36, 44–6, 51–3, 55–6, 86, 93–5, 114, 115, 124–5, 139, 140
contract gardening, 65, 66
Convallaria majalis, 19, 109
conversation pieces, 57
Cook, Captain James, 49, 69
Copenhagen, 137
Cordyline,
C. fruticosa, 59, **156**
C. terminalis, **156**
correa, 63
Costa Rica, 106
Cotyledon undulata, **157**
Country Life, 135
Cowell, John, *The curious and Profitable Gardener*, 39
cowslips, 115
Crassula arborescens, 59, 145, **156**
creeping jenny, 117
Crocus, 36, 43–5
C. vernus, 56, **154**
crocus pots, 'hedgehog', 56, 57
Croton. *See* Codiaeum
Crown imperial, 31, 43–4
Cruikshank, George, 65
'May - All A-Growing!', 80
Cyarthea princips, 96
Cyclamen, 130, 144
C. persicum, **155**
Cyperus alternifolius, 59, **156**
Cypher, James, 110

Daffodils, 42, 43–4, 45, 118
dahlias, 117, 118, 119
Daily Telegraph, 138
daisies, double, 46
Dampier, William, 31
dates, 22
Davidson, William 'Jock', 139
Delafield, E. M., *The Diary of a Provincial Lady*, 128
Delany, Mary, 41, 42, 48, 50, 51
Delftware, 33, 43
Denmark, 137, 138
Devonshire, 6th Duke of, 75, 127
Devonshire, 9th Duke of, 127
Dianthus, 66
    D. barbatus, 37, **155**
    D. caryophyllus, 18, 34, 119, **154**
    D. plumarius, 18, **154**
    'Souvenir de la Malmaison', **158**
Dibleys, 141
Dickens, Charles, *Pickwick Papers*, 113
Dickinson, Richard, 61
Dieffenbachia,
    D. bowmanii, **158**
    D. goldieana, **159**
    D. seguine var. *liturata*, **159**
dining room, 27, 42, 50, 66
display of plants, 65–6
Dominican Republic, 107
Doody, Mr, 32
Dracaena, 107, 127
    D. fragrans, **156**
    D. goldieana, **159**
    D. sanderiana, **159**
    D. surculosa, **157**
drawing rooms, 15, 33, 41, 50, 54, 56, 59, 60–2, 66, 77, 87, 95, 109, 110, 111, 115, 117, 126
Dreer, H. A., 123
dried flower arrangements, 111
Dumont's Insect Powder, 98–9
Duthie, Ruth, 119

Earle, Maria Theresa, 126
East London Observer, 119
Edmeades, Robert, 41
Edward I, King, 22
Edward, Prince of Wales (later King Edward VII), 109
Eleanor of Castile, Queen, 22
Elizabeth I, Queen, 17, 19
Encephalartos altensteinii, **156**
Endeavour, HMS, 69
Episcia cupreata, **158**
Erica, 66
    E. gentricosa, **156**
Erysimum cheiri, 18, 19, 24, 30, 36, 37, 63, **154**
Etruria, Staffordshire, 52, 53, 55

Euphorbia pulcherrima, 127, **157**
Evelyn, Charles, *The Lady's Recreation*, 32
Evelyn, John, 26–7, 27
    The Compleat Gard'ner (translation of La Quintinie), 35–6
    Kalendarium Hortense, 26
Evening Standard, 65
evergreens, 27
Exacum affine, **159**
exotics (tender plants), 21–3, 25–7, 31, 35, 39, 57, 63, 67, 73, 76, 81, 101–3, 126, 127, 146, 149

Facebook, 150, 151
Fairchild, Thomas, 30, 34–5, 39, 40, 79
    The City Gardener, 29, 33
Fairchild's Mule Pink, 34
Far East, 69, 140
Farrant, George, 60–1
Fatshedera lizei, 143–4
Fatsia japonica, 145
feng shui, 145
ferneries, 138
Ferns, 85, 91, 93, 97, 104, 105, 111, 117, 120, 125, 126
    fern mania, 92–3, 96
    Pteris, 130
Festival of Britain (1951), 133, 135
Fibrex, 141
Ficus, 97
    F. aspera 'Parcelli', **158**
    F. benghalensis, **155**
    F. benjamina, **156**
    F. elastica 'Decora', 135
    F. elastica indica, 126
    F. elastica, 72, 109, 126, 129, 135, 143, **157**
    F. lutea, **158**
    F. lyrata, 151
    F. microcarpa, **156**
    F. pumila, **155**
    F. religiosa, **156**
    F. robusta syn. *elastica*, 145
    F. rubiginosa, **156**
Fiennes, Celia, 27
figs, 22
Fiji, 72
Financial Times, 148
fireplaces, 13, 33, 34, 52, 93
First World War, 89, 123, 127
Firth, Captain, 62
Fittonia, *F. albivenis*, **159**
Flanders, weavers from, 37
Flanders, Michael, and Donald Swann, 134
floor, 29–30, 93
floor coverings, 24.
    See also carpets
floral motifs, 49–50

Floral World, 91
Floralies trade exhibition, Paris, British Plant and Greenhouse group, 140
Floricultural Society, 119–20
'Florist Feast', Norwich, 37
floristry, florists, 39–40, 109, 110
florists' flowers, 119
florists' societies, 118–19
flower arranging, 111, 128–9
flower bricks, 56
Flower Council of Holland, 146
flower de luce, 19
flower decoration, 128–30
flower market, 109
flower passage, 60
flower shows, 114, 116–18, 120, 146
flower stands, 55, 93–4
flowerpot covers, 95
flowers, cut, 11, 24, 35, 46, 53, 55, 108–9, 120, 124, 126–9, 135, 145–6
Flowers and Plants Association, 141
forcing, 14, 39–47
Forster, Johann sr and jr, 49
Forster, William, 110
fountains, 61, 105
Fowler's (pest control firm), 98
France, 125
Frankcom, Daniel, 33
Free, Montague, *All About House Plants*, 136
Frettingham's (pest control firm), 98
Fritillaria imperialis, 31, 43, **155**
    F. meleagris, 43
Frogmore House, Windsor, 61
Fuchs, Leonhart, 62
Fuchsia, 61–2, 87, 89, 96, 117, 120
    F. arborescens, 87
    F. coccinea, 61–2, **156**
    F. fulgens, 87, **158**
    F. magellanica, 87, **157**
    F. triphylla, 62, **155**
Furber, Robert, 39
    The Flower Garden Display'd, 41
Furber, William, 42
furnishing fabrics, with floral motifs, 49–50, 111
furniture, 49–51, 63–4, 86, 127
    garden, 93

Galium odoratum, 16
The Garden, 93, 95, 97, 148
Garden Centre Association, 148
garden centres, 146
garden cities, 127
gardeners,
    as staff, 82, 83
    hiring, 65, 66, 82

Gardeners' Chronicle, 105, 117
Gardeners' Company, 25
Gardener's Magazine, 71, 74, 80, 102, 118
Gardenia augusta, **156**
Garthwaite, Anna Maria, 50
gas fumes, 10, 84, 85, 110–11, 133
gas lighting, 84
Gentleman's Magazine, 81, 84
George V, King, 133
Geraniaceae, 77
Geraniums, 32, 63, 67, 76, 79, 113, 118, 126, 130
Gerard, John, 33, 37
    Herball, 21, 31
Germander, 13, 19
Gesneriads, 144
Gesnerias, 96
Gilbert, Richard, 136–7, 152
Gillies, Captain R., 71–2
Gillyflower, 18, 19, 37
Glasgow Botanic Garden, 70
Glasgow University, 70
glass, 35, 42, 44–6, 53, 59, 63, 72, 76, 92, 135
    tax on, 89
glass dome, 91
Gleichenia microphylla, 71
Glover, Mrs, 75
Gloxinia, 96, 135
Good Housekeeping, 134
Gosling, Mr, 61, 63, 146
Gothic Revival, 94
Grafton, Duke of, 103, 128
Grand Palm House, 73
Grant, Anne, 50
Great Exhibition (1851), 73, 94, 108
Great Fire of London, 29
greenhouses, 27, 41, 59, 61, 62–3, 86, 97, 101, 106, 109, 129
    miniature, 70–1, 85, 91
Grew, Nehemiah, 40
Groves, Mr, 120
The Guardian, 150
Gubb, Curtis, 152
Guzmania zahnii, 106

Hampton Court Palace, 16
Hanbury, Anna, 74
Harcourt, Lord, 41
Harrison, William, 15
Harrowby, 6th Earl of, 102
Hartlib, Samuel, 22
Harvey, John, 72
Hassard, Annie, 93
    Flower Decorations for Dwelling Houses, 128
Hatshepsut, Queen, 9
Haweis, Mary Eliza,
    The Art of Decoration, 90
Haworth, Adrian Hardy, 56

Haworthia,
    H. reinwardtii, **157**
    H. venosa subsp. *tesselata*, **157**
Haydon, George, 120
Heartsease, 66
Heaths, 130
heating, 16, 59, 133, 139, 147
Hedera, 141
    H. hibernica, 145
Helichrysum,
    H. bracteatum, 126
    H. stoechas, **155**
Heliotrope peruvianum, 54, **156**
Heliotropium arborescens, **156**
Henderson, Andrew, 76
Henry VI, King, 22
Henry VIII, King, 17
Hepatica, 43–4
herbs, 9, 14, 16–17, 19, 24, 44
Hesperis matronalis, 19
Hessayon, David, 137–8
    Be Your Own House Plant Expert, 138
Hibberd, James Shirley, 77, 90–2, 96, 101, 103, 105, 106, 107, 108, 110
    The Fern Garden, 92
    Rustic Adornments for Homes of Taste, 91, 120
Hibernia (ship), 71–2
Hibiscus, 21
    H. rosa-sinensis, **155**
    H. syriacus, 26
Hippeastrum,
    H. leopoldii, 32–3, **158**
    H. puniceum, 32
Hogarth, William, 57
Holder, Miss, 110
Holland, 9, 41, 51, 56, 140, 143
hollyhocks, 19
Honesty, 126
Honeysuckle, 37, 50
Hooker, Joseph Dalton, 72
Hooker, William Jackson, 72
Hopgood, Mr, 66
horticultural publishing, 90–1
Horticultural Society, 69, 75
Hortology, 150
hortus conclusus, 16
hortus fenestralis, 96
Hosta grandiflora, 125–6
hotbeds, 35, 46
hothouses, 39, 86, 101, 111, 124, 126, 127
The Housekeeper's Receipt Book, 82
houseplants, 133–41
    as term, 135
    health benefits, 144–5, 152
    popularity of, 148–53
housetop gardens, 97–8
Housewife, 138
Howea forsteriana, 76, 110, **159**

Hoya lanceolata spp. *bella*, 106, **158**
Huguenots, 37
Hunt, Elizabeth,
    Flora Domestica, 79
Hunt, J. H. Leigh, 79
Hyacinth, 36, 37, 40, 41–2, 42, 43–4, 45, 55, 119, 126
    double and triple, 41
    'Flora nigra', 41
    'Goldmine', 41
    Hyacinthus orientalis, **155**
    'King of Great Britain', 41
    'Ophir', 41
hybridization, 87, 144
Hydrangea, 96, 117, 127, 130
    H. macrophylla, **156**
hydroponics, 44, 140
Hylotelephium telephium, 13–14, **155**
Hypoestes phyllostachya, 143, **159**

Ideal Home, 134
IKEA, 149
imports, 51, 109, 130, 136, 152
India, 69, 72
Indian-rubber tree, 104
Industrial Revolution, 77
insects, insecticides, 82, 83, 98–9
Instagram, 150, 151
interior design, 49–51, 111, 124–30
International Year of Plant Health, 152–3
ipomeas, dwarf, 96
Iris, 19
    I. florentina, 18
    I. persica, 45
Italy, 26, 140
ivy, 30, 94, 96, 115

Jackson, John, 61, 63
Jacobsen, Arne, 138
Jade plant, 59
James I, King, 25
Japan, 74, 110
jardinières, 86, 95, 120, 125, 138
Jarrell, Cory, 152
jasmine, 39
Jasminum officinale, 37, **154**
Jekyll, Gertrude, 124–6
    Flower Decoration in the House, 124
John Innes Institute, 144
Johnson, Louisa, *Every Lady's Guide to her own greenhouse, hothouse and conservatory*, 82
Jones, Margaret E. and H. F. Clark, *Indoor Plants and Gardens*, 137, 138
jonquils, 36, 37, 42, 45
Jussieu, Joseph de, 53

Kalm, Per, 30
Kalosanthes, 117
Kamel, George Joseph, 74
Keats, John, 79
Kent, Elizabeth, 79–80, 81, 84
    Flora Domestica, 79, 87
Kentia palm, 76, 110, 130
Kik or Kirk, Everhard, 'Flower
    Album', 33
Kingsley, Charles, *Glaucus, or
    the wonders of the shore*, 92
Knossos, Crete, Minoan
    palace, 9
kokedama, 150
Kraunckwell, John and Mrs, 17

La Quintinie, Jean de, 35–6
Ladies' Magazine of Gardening,
    74, 75, 80, 84
Lancashire, 62
Lancaster, Osbert, 134, 137, 138
Lancaster, Roy, 134–5, 146
landscaping, 49, 60
Langley, Batty, *New Principles
    of Gardening*, 36–7
Lascelles, Mr, 97
Latania lontaroides, 73
Laurence, W. J. C., 144
Laurus nobilis, 19, **154**
Lavender, 16, 19
    Lavandula angustifolia, 16,
    18, **154**
Lee, James, 61, 62, 120
Lee and Kennedy, 76
Leeds, 114
    Bible Mission Room, 116
    St Andrew's Chambers, 115
    School Board, 114, 115
Leeds Ladies Educational
    Association, 114
Leeds pottery, 57
Lemnius, Levinus, 9, 15
lemon trees, 23, 59
Lemon verbena, 53–4
Letchworth Garden City,
    Hertfordshire, 127
Leucanthemum vulgare, **154**
Leyden Botanic Garden, 54
L'Heritier, Charles Louis, 39
light, 64, 83, 90, 96–7, 147
lighting, 149
    electric, 90
    gas, 84
Lilies, 34–5, 73
Lilies of the valley, 96, 109
Lilium candidum, **154**
Lindley, John, 75
Linnaeus, Carl, 21, 33, 39, 49, 74
Lithops, **157**
Lizé Frères nursery, Nantes, 143
Lobb, Thomas, 106
Lobb, William, 107
Loddiges, Conrad, 89, 92

Loddiges, George, 71, 72–4,
    75, 89
    The Botanical Cabinet, 143
Loddiges, Joachim Conrad,
    72–3
London,
    Aldermanbury, 30–1
    All Saints' Place, 95
    Bayswater, 66
    Beaufort House, Chelsea, 32
    Bethnal Green, 119
    Brompton Park Nursery, 31,
        35, 39
    Bryanston Square, 126
    Bunhill Row, Finsbury, 97
    Chelsea Flower Show, 146,
        153
    Chelsea Physic Garden, 32,
        40, 42, 53, 70
    Chiswick, 93
    Chiswick House, 75
    City of London Club,
        Old Broad Street, 96
    Connaught Square, 80
    Covent Garden, 56, 65, 69, 76,
        89, 109
    Crystal Palace, 73, 102
    Edgware Road, 79
    Eltham, 39
    Exotic Nursery, King's Road,
        Chelsea, 89
    Finchley, 89
    Finsbury Park, 120
    Fish Street Hill, 41
    Fulham, 108
    Golders Green, 61
    Hackney, 74, 92, 119, 120
    Hammersmith, 61
    Hampstead Garden Suburb,
        127
    Hampstead Heath, 79
    Highpoint flats, 127
    Holborn, 21
    Hoxton, 34
    Inner Temple, 119
    Kensington Gore, 42
    Kensington Nursery, 42
    Kensington Palace, 59
    Kew, Royal Botanic Gardens,
        31–2, 33, 49, 62, 69, 72, 75,
        92, 93, 115, 144
    King's Road, Chelsea, 76, 105
    Linley Sambourne House,
        Kensington, 96
    Little Coram Street, 116
    Loddige's Hackney Botanic
        Nursery, 73–4, 75, 76, 92
    Long Acre, 25
    Mayfair, 60, 130
    Mile End Road, 120
    Mile End, 119
    Mill Hill (formerly
        Middlesex), 79
    Old Ford, 119

Onslow Crescent, 108
People's Palace, Mile End
    Road, 120
Pine Apple Place, Edgware
    Road, 76
Poplar, 119
Regent's Park, 102
Roehampton, 61
Royal College of Art, 138
Soho, 51
Spitalfields, 50
St Bride's church, 43, 44
St George's parish,
    Bloomsbury, 116
St Martin's Lane, 13
Stoke Newington, 74, 104–5
Tottenham, 109
Tower Hamlets, 119, 120
Turnham Green, 84
University College, 75
Vineyard Nursery,
    Hammersmith, 76
Wapping, 62
Wellclose Square, 70
Westminster, 115
London, George, 31, 34, 35, 39
    and Henry Wise, *The Retir'd
    Gard'ner*, 34, 47
Lord Howe Island, 110
Loudon, Jane, 74, 80–7, 91
    *Instructions in Gardening
    for Ladies*, 81
Loudon, John Claudius, 55, 62,
    71, 76, 80–1, 83, 97, 103
    Encyclopaedia of Gardening,
    80
    Green-house Companion,
    62–5
Louis-Philippe, King, 102
Lovell, John, 17
*Low-Life: or One Half of the
    World...*, 57
Lunar Society, 84
lupin, 22
Lutyens, Edwin, 124, 126
Lybbe Powys, Mrs Philip, 41
Lychnis, 34
    L. chalcedonica, **154**
Lycopidium, *L. circinatum*, 73
Lye, James, 87
Lygodium, 96
    L. microphyllum, **157**
Lytocaryum weddellianum, **155**

Macmillan, Harold, 133
Maconochie, Alexander, 70
macramé, 138
Madagascar, 59
magazines and books,
    gardening, 90–1
magazines, women's, 138–9
Magnolia grandiflora, 126
mahogany, 50, 98, 127
maidenhair fern, 109

Malaya, 72
Maling, E. A., 94, 95–6, 98–9, 109
Indoor plants and how to grow them, 95
Malus,
M. 'Calville Blanche d'été', 37
M. 'Calville Rouge d'été', 37
Manet, Édouard, 101
Mangles, James, 66–7, 140
The Floral Calendar, 83
mantelpieces, 51, 55
Maranta leuconeura, 143, **159**
March, T. C., 103–4, 109
Flower and Fruit Decoration, 128
marigolds, 116, 117
marine motifs, 92
Marjoram, 9, 18, 19
Markham, Gervase, *The English Husbandman*, 16–17
Mason, L. Maurice, 144
Masson, Francis, 49
Matthiola incana, 19, **154**
Meager, Leonard, *The English Gardener*, 35–6
Medinilla magnifica, **158**
Ménagier de Paris, Le, 10
Mexico, 107
middle classes, 61, 74, 76, 80, 81–3, 86–7, 90–9, 102–4, 113–15, 126–8
Middleton, Lancashire, 37
Mignonette, 54–5, 57, 63, 67, 95, 96, 116, 117, 147
Mildmay, Grace, Lady, 17
Miller, Philip, 39, 42, 44, 54, 62
The Gardener's Dictionary, 40–1
Milton, Deborah, 24
Milton, John, 24
Mimosa, 104
M. pudica, **155**
Minton, Herbert, 94
Minton pottery, 94
Mirabilis jalapa, 44, **154**
mirrors, 51, 66
modernism, 127–30
Monstera, 151
M. deliciosa, 151
M. obliqua, 148
Moore, Charles, 110
Moore, Thomas,
A Handbook of British Ferns, 92
A Popular History of the British Ferns, 92
More, Sir Thomas, 41–5
Morris, Marshall, Faulkner and Company, 111
Morris, William, 111, 124
Moseley, Jonathan, 151
moss, 13, 64, 70, 86, 94, 104, 108, 115, 150

Mueller, Ferdinand, 110
musk, 96, 117
Myrrhis odorata, 16
myrtle, 30, 32, 34, 39, 63, 66, 79, 96
Myrtus communis, **154**

Narcissus, 19, 36, 37, 41, 42, 43–4, 45
N. jonquilla, **155**
N. pseudonarcissus, **154**
NASA, 145
nasturtium, 116
nemophilus, 96
neo-Georgian revival, 127
Nephrolepis exaltata 'Bostoniensis', **157**
Nerium oleander, **155**
nettle geraniums, 117
New South Wales, 110
New Zealand, 69
Nicol, Walter, 63–4
Nigella damascena, **155**
Nightingale, Florence, 85, 118
Norfolk, Duke of, 120
Norfolk and Norwich Horticultural Society, 118
North Africa, 24, 54
North America, 31.
See also Canada;
United States of America
Northamptonshire, 35
nosegays, 15, 45, 128
nurseries, nurserymen, 25, 65, 66–7, 69, 73, 76–7, 89, 105–7, 108–9, 110, 120, 135, 152

Oakes, Summer Rayne, 150
Ocimum basilicum, **154**
Old Windsor, Grove House, 54
oleander, 21
Olearia phlogopappa, 125
On the Growth of Plants in Closely Glazed Cases, 72
'On the Ledge', 150
Oncidium divaricatum, 73
Oncidium flexuosum, 73
Oplismenus hirtellus, **158**
Opuntia ficus-indica, **156**
orange mint, 44
Orange trees, 22–3, 26–7, 30, 34, 59, 60, 63, 66, 102, 106, 117
orangeries, 59
oranges, 18, 22
Orchids, 74–5, 97, 102, 106, 136, 144, 146, 149
epiphyrtic, 73
orchid fever, 75, 87
Oriental designs, 126
Origanum syriacum, 34
Orpin. *See Hylotelephium telephium*
orris root, 18

Oxford, 49
New College, 27
Physic Garden, 27
Oxford English Dictionary, 27, 93
oxygen, 84–5

paintings, 18, 24–5, 57, 129
palm-leaf fan, 111
palms, 73, 89, 105, 109, 110, 111, 124, 125, 126, 130
pampas grass, 111
Pan Britannica Ltd, 137, 138
Panama, 108
Pandanus veitchii, 107, 126, **158**
panelling, 15, 29, 51, 124, 127
pans and stands, 55, 93–4, 138
pansies, 96, 119
Paris, 54
Parkes, Revd Samuel Hadden, 116–18, 119
Window Gardens for the People, 118
Parkinson, John, 21–2, 24, 25–6, 33, 37
Paradisi in sole paradisus terrestris, 25, 26
parlours, 44, 45, 46, 50, 60, 64, 83, 93, 94, 105, 107, 110–11, 120, 128, 134, 145
Pascall's Patent Propagating Pot, 91
Pascall's West Kent Potteries, 91
Patch, 150
Paxton, Joseph, 73, 75, 102, 127
peach trees, 66
Pearce, Richard, 107–8
Pelargonium, 31, 39, 57, 76–7, 89, 103, 117, 120, 141
'Cape geraniums', 39
'Cooper's Scarlet', 77
'Frogmore Scarlet', 77
'General Tom Thumb', 77
'Huntsman', 77
P. betulinum, 39
P. capitatum, 31, **155**
P. ciconium inquinans, 77
P. ciconium zonale, 77
P. cordifolium, 49
P. cululatum, 39
P. echinatum, 49
P. fulgidum, **155**
P. grandiflorum, 49
P. indicum noctu odoratum, 31
P. inquinans, 31, **155**
P. panduriforme, 49
P. peltatum, 32, **155**
P. reniforme, 49
P. tomentosum, 49
P. triste, 31, **155**
P. zonale, **155**

Peperomia,
  P. argyreia, **158**
  P. magnoliaefolium, **157**
  P. obtusifolium, **156**
Pericallis x hybrida, **157**
Perrone, Jane, 150
Persian iris, 45
Peru, 54, 108
pests 98-9. *See also* insects
Petrie, Lord, 74
petunias, 117
phalaenopsis, 149
Philadelphia, 49, 123
Philippa, Queen, 10
Phillips, Mr, 110
Philodendron, 137
  P. melanochrysom, **159**
phlox, 22
Phoenix rupicola, 109
Phormium tenax variegata, **156**
photosynthesis, 85
Physalis alkekengi, 126
Pickard and Co., 95
Pickburn, J. T., 104–5
Pigett, W., 77
Pinks, 18, 30, 62, 117, 119
Pinterest, 150, 151
Pittosporum, 63
plague, 24, 29
plant breeders, 87
plant hiring, 110
plant hunting, 75, 89, 106, 147
plant labels, 137
plant screen (*Zimmerlaube*), 93
plant stands, 55, 93–4, 138
plants, living, benefits or ill
  effects within home, 84–5
Platt, Sir Hugh, 9, 11, 13–14,
  25, 39
  Delights for Ladies, 13, 17
  Floraes Paradise, 13–14
  *The Jewell House of Art and
  Nature*, 19
Platycerium bifurcatum, **157**
Plectranthus, 105
  P. fruticosus, **156**
Plumbago auriculata, **157**
Plumier, Charles, 107
  *Nova Plantarum
  Americanarum Genera*, 61–2
Poinsettia, 127, 140, 144
Polianthes tuberosa, **155**
polka-dot plants, 143
Polyanthus, 30, 36, 43, 45,
  46, 119
Polygala oppositifolia, 87
Polypodium vulgare, 126
pomanders, 18
Pomegranate, 22, 23, 102
Porcher, Felix, *Le Fuchsia, son
  histoire et sa culture*, 87
Portugal, 23, 26
pot covers, 95
pot pourri, 18, 53–4

pots, 43, 51–3
  double, 86
Potted Elephant nursery,
  Portland, Oregon, 152
Priestley, Sir Joseph, 84–5
primroses, 46, 115
  Chinese, 104
Primula, 96
  P. auricula, **155**
  P. obconica, **159**
  P. sinensis, **157**
  P. veris, 19
Prior, Charles, 123
privet, 34
propagation, 146, 149
Prunus spinosa 'Flore Plena',
  126
pteridology, 93
Public Health Act (1848), 89
Pugin, A. W. N., 94

Radnor, Earl of, 87
railways, 69
Raleigh, Sir Walter, 22
Ranunculus, 36, 37, 119, **155**
Rea, John, 23
Repton, Humphry, 60
  *Fragments on the Theory of
  Landscape Gardening*, 60
Reseda odorata, 54, **156**
respectability, 81, 113, 120
Rhododendron,
  R. formosum, **157**
  R. simsii, **157**
Richmond, Surrey, 17
Ricketts, George, 27
Rio de Janeiro, 71
Rishon, George, 55
Rivenhall, Essex, 19
Robinson, William, 93, 103,
  126
  The English Flower Garden,
  123–4
Robison, Sir John, 91
Rochdale, Lancashire, 37
Rochford, Betty, 140
Rochford, John, 109
Rochford, Michael, 109
Rochford, Thomas, 109
Rochford, Thomas III, 130,
  134, 135, 137, 140
Rochford Nursery,
  Hertfordshire, 109, 123–4,
  127, 130, 136, 139–41
  advisory service, 137
rockeries, 104–5, 111
Rolph, C. H., 120
Rome, ancient, 9
root pots, 53
rosemary, 16, 19
Roses (Rosa), 17, 50, 89, 96,
  118, 127
  R. damascena, 17
  R. gallica, 17

  R. rubiginosa, 37, **154**
Rosmarinus officinalis, 10,
  16, **154**
Rothschild, Lord, 120
Rousseau, Henri
  (Le Douanier), 128
Royal Botanic Society, Winter
  Garden, 102
Royal Doulton, 86
Royal Horticultural Society
  (RHS), 73, 93, 105, 146, 148,
  153
  'The Great Houseplant
  Takeover', 151
  garden centre, Wisley, Surrey,
  148, 151
  Grand Fruit and Flower
  Show, 105
  Harlow Carr, North
  Yorkshire, 151
  Houseplant and Cut Flower
  Advisory Group, 151
  Hyde Hall, Essex, 151
Royal Society of London, 40
Rubber plant. *See Ficus elastica*
Ruellia macrantha, **158**

St Albans, 13
St Paul-Illaire, Baron von, 136
Saint-Simon, Maximilien-
  Henri, Marquis de, *Des
  Jacintes...*, 55
Saintpaulia (African violet),
  135–6, 140, 143, 144
  'Endurance', 136
  S. confusa, 13
  S. ionantha, 136
  saintpaulia fever, 136
Saintpaulia and Houseplant
  Society, 135, 136, 146, 152
Salisbury, Richard Anthony, 79
Sanchezia speciosa, **158**
Sandon Hall, Staffordshire, 102
sanitary facilities, 89
Sansevieria trifasciata, 144
Santo Domingo, 107
Saxifraga fortunei, **158**
Scandinavia, 10, 133, 135, 138
scarlet runners, 116
scent, 9, 13, 17–19, 23, 24, 27,
  31, 37, 41, 53–6, 76, 101–2,
  106, 147
Schefflera,
  S. elegantissima, **158**
  S. veitchii, **158**
Schlumberg, Frederick, 143
Schlumbergera, 143
Scindapsis, 137
Second World War, 130, 133
seeds, importing, 130, 136
Selaginella, 97, 108
  S. denticulata, 93, 109
  S. kruassiana, **159**
self-watering system, 14

servants, 12, 27, 63, 76, 81–2, 85, 103, 117, 133
Seven Years' War, 69
Sèvres factory, 57
sewage control, 89
Shakespeare, William, 18, 19
Shelley, Percy Bysshe, 79
Sherard, James, 39
Sherard, William, 32
Shoults and Kay, 89
Shrewsbury Flower Show, 123
shrubs, 19, 24–5, 33, 74, 106, 124, 126, 129
sick building syndrome, 145
silk, Spitalfields, 50
The Sill, 150
Simond, Louis, 51, 55
Singapore, 144
Sinningia speciosa, **157**
Sloane, Sir Hans, 33, 107
Smith (apothecary), 30–1
snowdrops, 36, 43–4, 56, 115
Solanum, 89, 125
Solenostemon, *S. scutelarioides*, 105, **156**
Sollya heterophylla, **87**
The Somerset House Conference, 24–5
Song, Jamie, 150
South Africa, 31, 105
South America, 21, 49, 72, 75
South Pacific, 49
Southwell, Mr and Mrs, 52
Spain, 26
Sparmannia africanana, **156**
Spathiphyllum, *S. wallisii*, 144, **159**
spider plant, 138–9, 145
Spiraea japonica, 125
Spry, Constance, 130
staging, 63–4
Stanley, Arthur Penrhyn, Dean, 118
Stanley, Lady Augusta, 115, 118
Staphylea colchica, 125
Stephanotis floribunda, **157**
still rooms, 17
stocks, 30, 36, 37, 66, 117
Stoke-on-Trent, 94
stove houses, 35, 59, 82, 86, 107
strawberries, 117
Strelizia reginae, **156**
Streptocarpus, 135, 141, 144
'Constant Nymph', 144
S. biflorus, 106
S. gardenii, **158**
S. polyanthus, **158**
S. rexii, 144, **157**
Sturgeon, Andy, 143, 145
succulents, 127, 150
Sunday Times, 148
supermarkets, 137, 145
sweet briar, 37, 66
sweet peas, 63

Sweet, Robert, 76–7
Sweet William, 30, 34
Sweet woodruff, 16
Sydney, Australia, 71
syngium, 137

tables, 15, 24, 50, 60, 64, 66, 93, 140
Tanzania, 143
tea crop, 72
technology, 10, 51, 62, 69, 72, 84, 90, 147, 149
television, 10, 90, 134, 137
tender plants. *See* exotics
terracotta, 9, 36, 57, 139
terrariums, 150
Thomas, Maya, 153
Thornden Hall, Essex, 74
Thornton, Peter, 86
Thrower, Percy, 137
Thunbergia mysorensis, 106
thyme, 16
Thymus serpyllum, 16
Thymus vulgaris, 16
The Times, 118
Tissot, James, 101
Titanic, RMS, 123
tobacco, 22
Tod, George, 61, 63
Todea superba, 96
tomatoes, 22
tools, 98
Tower Hamlets Floricultural Society, 119
Chrysanthemum Show, 119
Tradescant, John the Elder, 21, 22, 31
Tradescant, John the Younger, 21, 22
Tradescantia,
T. fluminensis, **157**
T. spathacea, **156**
T. virginiana, 21
T. zebrina, **158**
Transactions of the Horticultural Society of London, 56
transport, 69–70, 71, 127, 147
Treiwald, Samuel, 41, 44
'An Account of Tulips and other Bulbous Plants...', 40
trellis, 138
Tuberose, 21, 34, 35
Tübingen, 62
tufa, 103–4
Tulipa (tulips), 36–7, 40, 41, 43–4, 45, 62, 116, 119, **155**
Turnford Hall estate, Hertfordshire, 109
Tusser, Thomas, *Five Hundred Points of Good Husbandry*, 19
tussie-mussies, 18

Umbrella Plant, 59
United States of America, 21–2,

31, 49, 74, 123, 136, 137, 143, 146, 150. *See also* South America
Usambara Mountains, Tanzania, 136

van Royen, Adrian, 54
Veitch, Harry, 93
Veitch, James, the Elder, 89
Veitch, James, Jr, 106
Veitch, John Gould, 107
Veitch nursery, 105–7, 108, 109
ventilation, 84–5, 146
verbena, 66, 117
Verney, Sir John, 21
Viburnum tinus, **154**
Victoria, Queen, 89, 94, 109, 120
Victoria Regia (amazonica), 73
Vincent, Alice, 153
Viola odorata, **154**
Viola tricolor, **154**
Violets, 36, 84, 96, 115
Neapolitan, 126
Virginia creeper, 116
Voerhelm, Pieter, 41
Voysey, C. F. A., 124

wall hanging, 50
Wallflower.
See Erysimum cheiri
wallpaper, 49–50, 51, 111
Ward, Nathaniel Bagshaw, 69–73, 75, 84, 89, 90
Wardian cases, 69–73, 85–6, 91–3, 95, 96, 105, 110, 111, 120, 126, 138
water supplies, 29, 51, 73, 147
watering, 44–6, 63, 82–3, 139, 140, 146
Weatherall, Richard, 89
Wedgwood, Josiah, 51–3, 55, 56–7, 84
Wedgwood (firm), 86
wells, 29
Wendland, Hermann, 136
West Indies, 33, 69
Westminster, Duchess of, 120
William I (the Conqueror), King, 18
William III, King (William of Orange), 31, 41
Wills & Segar, 108–9, 109
Willson, Mr, 77
Wiltshire, 87
Windebank, Sir Thomas, 23
window boxes, 19, 32, 54, 55, 57, 62, 67, 114
self-watering system, 14
'Window Gardening for the Poor' movement, 116–19
window gardens, 116–19
window tax, 30, 51
windows, 29–30, 50
double, 96

windowsills, 11, 17, 19, 30, 43, 45, 46, 50, 70, 76, 77, 113, 120, 126, 136, 143, 144, 146
winter gardens, 96–7, 102, 108
Wise, Henry, 31, 34, 35, 39
Woburn Abbey, Bedfordshire, 27
Wolsey, Cardinal Thomas, 18
Wolverhampton, Pearsall Cottage, 75
Wolverton, Dr B. C., 145
Woman's Own, 134, 139

women,
and houseplants, 141
as horticulturalists, 81–2, 98
as visitors to flower shows, 120
employed in nurseries, 127
magazines, 138–9
role post-Second World War, 133, 134
Wong, James, 150, 151
working classes, 62, 113, 115, 119–20
Worlidge, John, 24, 27

Yonge, Charlotte, The Daisy Chain, 101, 103
Yorkshire Post, 114
Yorkshire School of Cookery, 114

Zahn, Gottlieb, 106
Zamioculca, Z. zamiifolia, 143, 144
Zanzibar, 143
Zimmerlaube, 93
'Zonals', 76

ACKNOWLEDGEMENTS

I am enormously indebted to Jo Christian and all at Pimpernel Press for allowing me to update this book in view of the exciting developments in the houseplant world in the last decade. Editor Anna Sanderson and designer Becky Clarke were the perfect team – full of inspiration and patience. In addition to all the people mentioned below who assisted me with the original edition, I would particularly like to add thanks to Jane Perrone for her help with the revisions and Christopher Woodward, director of the Garden Museum, and Alice Vincent for their continual support and promotion of the book over the years.

I remain grateful for the all generous help I received in preparing the original text. Thanks go to supreme plantsman Roy Lancaster, Brent Elliott and staff at the RHS Lindley Library, Carla Teune of the Hortus botanicus, Leiden, Veronica Richardson and all at The Plant and Flower Association, Ed Woolf of Indoor Garden Design, Thomas Rochford, Michael Loftus of Woottens of Wenhaston, Jim Read of Read's Nursery, Martin Panter of Arnott & Mason, New Covent Garden, Sam Youd of Tatton Park and Colleen Smith. Once again, I would like to thank Christine Lalumia, formerly of the Geffrye Museum for all her support, Lynn Miller of the Wedgwood Museum, Clare Brown of the Victoria and Albert Museum, Peter Brown, former director of Fairfax House, York, Paula Henderson, Eve Setch, Amanda Vickery, Hannah Greig, Jane Hamlett, Rebecca Preston, Ruth Gorb, and staff at the many museums and libraries I made use of, in particular, the London Library and the RIBA Library. I am particularly grateful to Charlotte Gere, Patricia Ferguson and Julia Matheson for advice and access to their work which was invaluable.

Finally, I will always be indebted to the late Richard Gilbert, past President of the Saintpaulia and Houseplant Society, for sharing with me a little of his encyclopaedic knowledge on indoor plants.

'Design for Living' from At the Drop of a Hat by Flanders & Swann (1956) by permission of the Estates of Michael Flanders & Donald Swann.

All illustrations are from the author's collection.